"In this fasci⬚ ⬚⬚⬚ sub-
cultures, How ⬚⬚⬚⬚ ⬚sual
but real life i⬚ a vivid expose of human dignity, pain,
doubt, uncertainty, injustice, and survival. Through it
all, he emerges blessed with forgiveness and a Christian
belief system that embraces humanity with love, compas-
sion, empathy, and selflessness.

Howard provides insight into a sub-culture in the
United States that evolved partially due to the freedoms
we enjoy and the rights we have to practice our faiths.
These freedoms sometime lead humans to manipulate
and control family, children, and friends. It is the human
dilemma. It is the challenge we face with and from one
another, our religion, our government, friends, and foes.
It is the reason our forefathers created the separation of
powers in the formation of the USA. They realized that
centralized power over human beings leads invariably
to manipulation, control, and often abuse. This occurs in
sub-cultures as well, and is what Howard experienced in
his youth. It is a lesson we do well to learn from.

Through it all, Howard survived to share a very
real experience that many of us could not imagine. The
personal and emotional feelings he shares throughout
Addicted to Certainty are ones only a person who has
experienced them can relate to.

This book is an important read for anyone, as it
exhibits what has occurred over many generations and
countries throughout the evolution of human culture. It
reaches in and touches the human soul and shares that
survival and overcoming are possible!"

Kurt Grimmer, *Financial Advisor, Legacy
Capital Partners; Commissioner, PenMet Parks*

"Journeys. We are all on one. How is your journey going? Are you enjoying it? Making progress?

Addicted to Certainty, written by my friend, Howard Mackert, is the story of a very unique and unusual journey. Do you want to move forward in your own journey? Reading (and considering) Howard's journey will help you on yours.

You will find yourself saying things like, 'Wow!' and 'Really?' and, 'Oh, my!' You will laugh and you will wonder. And, even though his journey is very different from yours in some ways, you will find yourself related to it and growing because of it."

Dennis Fuqua, *Director, International Renewal Ministries; Former Pastor, Peninsula Christian Fellowship*

"What a life Howard Mackert has lived! Howard introduces us to his story as a 'plyg kid,' brought up in a fundamentalist Mormon family made up of one husband, four wives, and twenty-seven kids. It is a journey told sympathetically but realistically, 'written from a place of healing and forgiveness,' as he puts it.

Howard's story is a compelling page-turner, largely because of his transparency and honesty as our guide into this strange-yet-familiar world. It's a story that gives us keys to how a wounded person can boldly and graciously come to terms with a difficult past.

Addicted to Certainty portrays a way of life that could easily be sensationalized and painted in cartoonish strokes. But Mackert invites us into his story with a sober and honest narrative. In an age where we can be tempted to hate and dehumanize others, this book models a way that accepts the ambiguity and tensions found in real life. We don't have to be addicted to certainty. Rather, we can accept the world as it is, full of uncertainty, and embrace our neighbors, family members, and even the stranger with all of their good and bad traits, all of their beauty and flaws."

Larry Ciccarelli, *Translation Consultant, SIL International*

"Howard takes us from the chains and suffering of fundamentalism to embracing the sweet mystery of his own spirituality. Leaving behind his 'addiction to certainty,' Howard gives us the courage to find our own way to God. He shows us we have the ability to discover, in our hearts, the love and peace we need, and to share it with those we love."

Dan Cohen, *Artist and Educator at Bellarmine Preparatory School*

"*Addicted to Certainty* gives the reader hope and understanding for those who are born into circumstances that do not encourage freedom and personal choice. Howard courageously shares his journey in finding self-worth and peace. I believe this book can help others who may find themselves in similar circumstances. Whether it be a religion, a relationship, or a job, this book shows how following your heart and living your life with love, acceptance, and true grace brings peace and happiness."

Julie Thomson, *Owner, Family First Adult Family Homes*

ADDICTED
TO
CERTAINTY

PAM :)

HOPE MY STORY MAKES
YOU LAUGH + CRY.

ENJOY, Howard

ADDICTED

TO

CERTAINTY

The Journey of a
Twice-Recovering Fundamentalist

HOWARD C. MACKERT

Addicted to Certainty: The Journey of a Twice-Recovering
Fundamentalist
First Edition, 2020
Copyright © 2020 by Howard C. Mackert

To order additional books:
www.amazon.com
www.addictedtocertainty.com

ISBN: 978-1-7332679-4-6
Editorial and Book Packaging: Inspira Literary Solutions, Gig
Harbor, WA
Book Design: PerfecType, Nashville, TN
Cover Design: Brianna Showalter, Ruston, WA
Printed in the USA by Ingram Spark

*I'm pleased to dedicate this book to my awesome wife,
Rhonda, who has taught me so much and
endured the less than desirable versions of me
up to this day.
Thank you, Babe; I'm crazy about you.*

*I also want to dedicate this book to my amazing mom.
I used to tell people that each one of
her eleven children would swear
they were her favorite, until I said that
in front of a handful of siblings,
at which they started to laugh. Apparently they all knew I was her favorite;
they recognized it but I felt it—I just
thought it was universal!
To my confidante, friend, coach, and life teacher:
I love you, Midge Mackert, to the moon.*

Acknowledgments

This book would never have happened without the exceptionally professional guidance of Arlyn Lawrence, owner of Inspira, my book editor and producer. She knows the flow and structure of books like I know engines. She did the seasoning of my words to give them impact and meaning. I wasn't a writer (although I guess you'd have to say I am once this book is published!), and I was committed to putting out a high-quality manuscript—and Arlyn has made that happen.

A special thank you to my amazing family, not just my full brothers and sisters, but my equally important half-siblings. We never talked that way about each other, but I want to clarify that for my readers. They are all sacred friends who have a common history, struggle, and hopes, and varied successes. As adults, we have become close friends with an amazing bond.

I want to express my appreciation to my crew at Mackert Automotive LLC, who first of all do an excellent job of representing me to our "crazy cool" community of Gig Harbor. They make me look good. They carry on while I'm behind a closed office door clunking away on the keyboard.

A special acknowledgment to two college professors: first of all, Jim Cotts, the Dutchman, my math mentor/ professor in college, who would give me the worst time if a chemistry major outscored me on a test. He put me in the choir at the only Presbyterian church in Cedar City, Utah and that was my first exposure to non-Mormons.

The second professor of influence was my choir and vocal coach, Ron Aden. His family was going to the church that Heidi took me to early on. They put up with my transition mistakes, and I learned so much there musically.

I should also mention Ron and Wanda Thompson, who came down from Northern Utah to plant a new church north of Cedar City, and were so patient with me.

I must include my father-in-law, Dee L. Odell. He was my "Christian father," who loved me like his own son. His quiet strength anchored me through difficult times. I always knew he was on my side, encouraging me along the way. We shared the joy of all things mechanical, including motorcycles, airplanes, cars, and racing of almost any kind. I'll never forget when we bought him a tandem hang-gliding flight for his sixtieth birthday. He was like a little kid getting his first pony ride. He was strong and childlike at the same time, something I hope rubbed off on me.

And finally, I want to acknowledge the input of several writers whose wisdom impacted me tremendously in my life, and whose books opened my eyes to another way of thinking while I was deep in fundamentalism:

- C.S. Lewis, the brilliant man who read Greek like his mother tongue, which allowed him to understand the subtleties and humor written in the New Testament. His insights and books were life-altering to me. His imagination is a gift to Christianity and all those who want to become followers of Jesus.
- George MacDonald, the twentieth-century Scottish theologian who was too radical in his writings to find a place in the Church at his time. His "Unspoken Sermons" are so deep it took multiple readings of many to grasp what he was saying. I've never before found a page-long sentence that packs so much truth and wisdom.
- A.W. Tozer, a Chicago pastor and brilliant communicator of truth and wisdom. His books caused some of the earliest cracks in my "fundamentalist wall."
- Brian McLaren, and my friend Robert Wormley who introduced me to him. I am so grateful for his insight into how modern thinking—with its binary modes of "on or off," "in or out"—had influenced my worldview, as well as the Church as I'd

experienced it. He helped me see a better way of evaluating the writings of others.

- Wm. Paul Young, author of *The Shack*. That book rocked my world! It rewrote my software with a view of God that pushed me over the edge into all-out love! Rhonda will tell you that she would come out of the bedroom in the mornings and find me sobbing uncontrollably or belly laughing at what I'd just read. The thought that God was "especially fond of me" penetrated my soul and set me free from fear. Thank you, my friend.

TABLE OF CONTENTS

"We may be content to remain what we call ordinary people, but He is determined to carry out a quite different plan. To shrink back from that plan is not humility; it is laziness and cowardice. To submit is not conceit or megalomania; it is obedience."

—C.S. Lewis

Introduction

Many of you may have seen the HBO series *Sister Wives,* or perhaps have seen or read the growing number of articles, books, and testimonies published by and about polygamy survivors. There has been much in particular written recently about Warren Jeffs, the leader (although from prison now) of the polygamist sect Fundamentalist Church of Jesus Christ of Latter-Day Saints (FLDS).

Because of all the hype already out there on this topic, I want my readers to know from the start this is not a "tell-all"-type book. I have no axe to grind, just a unique story to tell. Frankly, I've read some of those books and felt like I needed a shower afterward, even skipping some of the more graphic chapters. This book is not that way.

This is a story written from a place of healing and forgiveness. I have no hatred or resentment toward anyone for the things done to me and pray no one has hard feelings toward me for my part in what has happened. From our earliest years, we were told to "obey and follow the prophet," and our salvation would be assured. That is a hard thing for a young person to refute or resist when they've grown up in a controlling culture like we did, and have little context for understanding any other way. It's also a powerful cocktail for anyone who wants to abdicate personal responsibility.

If you're looking for shock literature, this is not it. It is instead a chronicled journey of an insignificant little boy and his struggle for significance. As one of twenty-seven full and half-siblings, and four step-siblings, it was very difficult in our household not to feel like just a number. I gave my dad an intellectual pass for not being there; with four wives and thirty-one children; how could he? But inside me was a little boy who longed to be held and given affection from his father.

That longing fueled a lifelong, all-consuming desire to win. If I could just be good enough, my dad would notice me. I would mean something to him; I might even get an encouraging word of praise. It was a problem that did not pass with my adolescence; even when he was a thousand miles away, I still had to win at all costs.

Over the years, I've learned that a little bit of me goes a long way with some people. But because I've learned to truly love myself, warts and all, I no longer feel the need to re-invent myself or put on a mask to make myself more palatable to them. The tricky part is to not look down on them as deficient or wrong because they don't like me, which I believe is our most normal tendency (though an unhealthy one).

I have now grown to the point that I can appreciate even the "bad" things that happened to me, because all those events contributed to who I am today. Take away any of those steps and I wouldn't be the same. The suffering I've experienced—that we all experience in various means and degrees—has taught me to "weep with those who mourn." It has taught me to empathize, not just sympathize, with people in pain. How else do you learn that?

I hope my story helps you, too, learn to resolve and even embrace all that comes (or has come) your way. If we all do, we can maximize the lessons learned. Maybe if we learn quickly, we won't have to "take that test" repeatedly—that is, we don't have to continue to prove ourselves, over and over again, to a standard or a person that exists only in our own mind.

The way most of us think in the Western world is linear. It's like making a salad, piece by piece. When you're done and it's all mixed up, you can still make out the individual parts. But, in my view, life is more like a good stew; you add ingredients (your experiences), and, as they cook, they lose their unique flavor. They combine with the other ingredients and create a beautiful flavor unattainable by themselves. I believe that is why we must put to use everything that comes into our lives—the good and the bad—because it is all necessary to produce the people we are today.

I also believe that unforgiveness over the past spoils the stew. There is a universal truth that when we hold on to bitterness, it is like drinking poison and hoping the other person dies. The only one it really hurts is us.

As you continue reading this book, you'll discover the process I went through to forgive both my father and myself—and how I discovered the unconditional love and acceptance that changed my life forever. This book is an expression of that process in my life, and I hope it helps you, my reader, in a similar way.

Howard Mackert
Gig Harbor, Washington
2020

CHAPTER ONE

Plyg Kid

I grew up in Salt Lake City, under the shadow of the LDS temple. At least 90 percent of the students in our high school were LDS (Church of Jesus Christ of Latter-Day Saints, aka the Mormon Church). The next highest population after the regular Mormons was made up of the polygamists. That was us—hence, the nickname "plyg kids."

I went to Jordan High School in Sandy, Utah, along with the now-infamous Jeffs Clan. Rulon Jeffs had a compound with high walls around a 10,000-square-foot home at the mouth of Little Cottonwood Canyon. Oddly, this region also hosts the entrance to the Snow Bird and Alta ski resorts, "the best snow on earth." How could a region so strikingly beautiful also be so strikingly strange? The last numbers I heard were that Rulon Jeffs had twelve wives and seventy-two children.

There were a lot of different-looking Jeffs at our school, and then there were us Mackerts. We dressed the same (picture *Little House on the Prairie*), but lacked the status of blue-blood polygamists like the Jeffs. Even in our little twisted corner of the world, we were looked down on by the majority.

———

My mother had been converted to Mormonism (specifically the polygamist version of Mormonism) many years earlier by a woman in Casper, Wyoming. When my dad got out of the Army and returned home, Mom met him at the door with a Book of Mormon in her hands and drew a line in the sand: accept it or lose his family. He accepted it—which made us converts, second generation. That could not compare to the Jeffs' history, which went back to the Brigham Young days.

Rulon Jeffs was what they called an "apostle" of the FLDS (Fundamentalist Latter-Day Saints). He owned an accounting firm in town and, like most FLDS, his wives and children worked to help with the family's finances. Rulon built a huge home with a one hundred by twenty-five-foot meeting room that was used by the Salt Lake City "saints" as a meeting place every Sunday afternoon. My father's wives each had their own home until I was in the eighth grade, and we took turns meeting at one of them for our combined morning Sunday school-type class. After that, we shared a quick lunch and were off to the Jeffs' compound for a group meeting.

When I was young, there were seven apostles in the leadership, with Rulon being the most newly appointed and youngest. However, by the early eighties, there were only four left alive and no new appointments had been made. A rumble started going through the group about whether or not any apostle could receive revelation for the group or only the president, who held the keys to the priesthood. The latter group became known as the "One-Man Doctrine" group and included the current President, Leroy Johnson, and Rulon Jeffs. The other two remaining apostles left or were kicked out; either way, they moved across the highway to Centennial Park and started up their own little community.

This new sect allowed individuals to own their own land, so soon beautiful homes started popping up. Their women were allowed to wear modern clothes and even make-up. The group also did away with pre-arranged marriages, allowing the women to be courted by prospective suitors.

When Leroy Johnson died, Rulon Jeffs took over leading the "chosen seed" (or "frozen seed," as we all called them). In many instances, they looked down on us

Mackerts, in the hierarchy of who was in and who was out. So, we were spurned by the normal kids and also by the ones we were most like, which really sucked.

———

I was one of the "triplets" in my family, so-called because my dad fathered three boys born in the span of eleven days. It was such a male-dominant culture that the birthing mothers were almost an afterthought. I heard stories of how proud my dad was to have three strapping boys so close together.

It was all about the men: they held the priesthood, and had all the authority. The women acted under the authority of their husband, even in disciplining young ones. There is strong incentive in the FLDS for these women to toe the line. In Mormon theology, the man calls the wife from the grave in the afterlife, so they must keep him happy if they even want to wake up in the next life.

These teachings are part of the original LDS teachings, so don't go to your Mormon neighbor or friend and ask them about this; they probably have never heard of it. Only 10 percent of baptized Mormons are even allowed in the temple. Going through the temple requires a "temple recommend" from the local bishop, which states that the faithful participant tithes 10 percent or more faithfully, attends all the regular and special priesthood meetings, and regularly donates time to church projects.

In the temple, "deeper truths" are revealed and initiates are strongly warned against divulging any details. A temple marriage includes a time when the bride and groom are separated and the man is told his "Adamic name" (his name in heaven) and his wife's name. The wife is only told *her* heavenly name, not her husband's.

Besides that, the Mormons have an interesting theology that "the living prophet is worth any ten dead ones." This comes from their utter belief that their current prophet is the oracle of God for this earth. That's why they had no problem when, in 1890, Wilford Woodruff received a "revelation" that polygamy was no longer required to enter the highest level of heaven and become a god over your own planet.

"The highest level of heaven" refers to Mormon Church founder Joseph Smith's theology of heaven, which was loosely based on the apostle Paul's reference (in the Bible) to being "caught up to the third level of heaven."[1] Smith picked up on that phraseology and taught that there are three realms in heaven.

First, he asserted, is the "Telestial Kingdom," which is considered to be the lowest level and reserved for people who never heard the restored truth, and weren't very

---

1. See 2 Corinthians 12:2

good on this earth. I should add that, in this view, hell is reserved for murderers and "sons of perdition" or apostates. So if someone hasn't turned away from the truth or killed anyone, they will not go to hell, per se.

The second heaven, Smith taught, is the "Terrestrial Kingdom," reserved for the honorable men and women of this earth who didn't get to hear the restored truth—for example, Ghandi, Mother Theresa, maybe your favorite uncle or aunt, and, of course Mormons who don't qualify for the "Celestial Kingdom."

To qualify for the Celestial Kingdom, the third heaven, a Mormon has to be married in the temple, serve a two-year mission, work in the temple, be baptized for the dead, and fulfill other demands of time and money. If you live a righteous life, you will be resurrected into the Celestial Kingdom and be allowed to have multiple goddess wives. Only the faithful who reach this level are resurrected with any ability to procreate; the rest are eunuchs. In heaven, if you make it into that elect group, you will have celestial sex and produce spirit children to populate the planet you will create. You will, in essence, be a god. In fact, Mormons have a saying that, "As man is, God once was. And as God is, man may become."

At least, that's what we were told.

———

But, I digress. Woodruff's revelation in 1890 was that polygamy was no longer required to enter the highest level of heaven and become a god over your own planet. It should be noted that this "revelation" was heavily motivated by that fact that a large contingent of the U.S. army was camped on the eastern side of the Salt Lake Valley, ready to put the whole territory of Utah under martial law for practicing polygamy. The announcement of the new revelation stayed the hand of the government and a few years later, on January 4th, 1896, Utah became the forty-fifth state in the United States.

As you can imagine, many of the established polygamist families were outraged and wondered if the church would take away parts of their family. Several of the twelve apostles of Mormon leadership, who had many wives themselves, got together secretly in order to see to it that no year passed without a child being born under the "principle of celestial marriage," as polygamy was called.

Lorin Calvin Wooley, John Taylor, and others headed up this effort. They quickly became known as "fundamentalists," adhering to the original teachings of Joseph Smith and Brigham Young. I mention Lorin Wooley's middle name because I was born on his birthday, October 23rd, and was given his middle name, Calvin. My younger brother Shem, born two days later, has the middle name Lorin.

In the early 1940s, several of these founding families bought a chunk of land on the Utah and Arizona border, called "Short Creek." All the land was titled to the "United Effort Plan," or UEP, which meant the church owned the land. This has led, even to this day, to decades of poverty and deplorable living conditions because no one can get a mortgage or construction loan, since they don't own the land on which they are building.

The homes are like an onion in reverse, many starting with a mobile trailer somewhere in the center. Additions are paid for as they can be afforded, so most homes have no landscaping and no siding, just black tar paper. Only the richest homes look even close to finished. My mom actually lived in a "cleaned-out" stinky old chicken coop when they first moved there.

These fundamentalists were in obvious rebellion against the established Mormon leaders, and it was not taken lightly. Anyone caught was excommunicated by the LDS leadership. We, however, were never members of the LDS church. Most LDS resented polygamists because of the reminder of their own embarrassing history. It didn't help that polygamists believe that when the mainstream Mormon church gave up polygamy, they lost the priesthood and were apostatized. So, not only were we different, we had an elitist attitude that really rubbed them the wrong way.

We were taught that when Joseph Smith and Jesus return to Earth together to set the Church in order before the final judgment, they will go to Salt Lake City and restore the polygamist fundamentalists' access to temple ceremonies and rituals. We believed everyone outside of our circle of belief were "Gentiles" (a term borrowed from Jewish spiritual roots), and we were not allowed to associate with them unless absolutely necessary. We were the only ones with the truth, the only ones going to the highest of the three levels of heaven, and the only ones who would ultimately become gods of our own planets.

CHAPTER TWO

"Keep Sweet"

If you've seen any pictures or footage of polygamists in the media, you might think you were watching old history, mostly because of the way we dressed. Any young person will tell you that clothes are extremely important in school and almost all of mine were homemade, or hand-me-down AND homemade. The only clothes not homemade were our underclothes, blue jeans, socks, and shoes. Once I was out of school, my mom even made me long underwear to mimic the temple garments worn by the faithful FLDS!

The original temple garments were ankle to wrist and just under the chin. So, we had to wear long-sleeved shirts buttoned all the way up and long pants. My sisters made most of their own clothes, and dresses had to be just above the ankle as well. These days that would stand out like an alien from Mars, and it pretty much did back then, as well.

When I was in high school, the standard for all the students was that we couldn't have hair that touched our collars (and we always had to wear shirts with collars). No shorts were allowed either, and girls had to have skirts no higher than mid-thigh (remember, my sister's skirts were barely above their *ankles*). To say we stood out is a huge understatement.

Before I started the eighth grade, we moved into a house on six acres, complete with a barn, cows, horses, and a full-acre garden. Before that we had three houses for most of my life, then four when my dad married a woman with four children (two boys and two girls), bringing our family count to thirty-one children. Because we were living in three houses in different parts of town, we triplets all started in different school districts, resulting in David, the oldest, and Shem, the youngest, starting school one year before me. It was strange to be in driver's education with them and being in different classes. The teachers quickly caught on that we had three different moms.

After my eighth grade year, when David and Shem were going into high school (we had a three-year high school system), an effort was made to get me double promoted so I would be in sync with them in school. However, the school superintendent had an older brother who had been double promoted and later went crazy, and felt those circumstances were clearly related. That sealed my separateness from my brothers, and my self-perception as being second fiddle. Even though I was their age, I felt less than, not good enough, inferior.

My tenth grade year was not unlike the others', except my younger sisters were still in middle school, so I didn't have them tagging along as we walked to school and back. As a kid, I was given the nickname "Huck." My brothers would tease me with it, calling my sisters "Huck's heifers." I would walk ten yards in front of them, but no further or I would get in trouble with Father for not being close enough to protect them. Those were humiliating days. I can only imagine how bad it was for my sisters.

Like most school systems, there was more than one middle school that fed into the high school, so there were quite a few students who didn't know me as that kid who had sisters who dressed oddly. It was like a new start in many ways.

There was a cute girl in my biology class who happened to be the captain of the cheerleading squad. She sat three rows in front of me and one seat over; she was stunning. I told the teacher I couldn't see the board from where I was, so he had me move forward right next to her—score! She acted as if she liked me, but I suspected she was just being nice to me out of pity, like the girls who were kind to the mentally impaired kids. That's how deep my insecurities ran.

I was always very good in school and with my help she passed the class. Once she even invited me to stop by her house some time, but of course I couldn't associate with Gentiles and had to say no. One more layer of shame! I wasn't normal, I didn't fit in, I hated my life! But of course, I couldn't let it show, so I put on a smile and went about my plyg kid life. "Keep sweet," they told us.

———

At a young age, we were taught to lie about our parent's lifestyle. If asked if we were polygamists, we responded, "That's funny, I heard that about *your* dad." That would put them on the defensive, to say the least.

We also didn't celebrate Christmas; who could blame our parents, with that many children? Someone decided that Jesus had been born on April 6th, not December 25th, and that settled the matter.

Father taught us how to deflect questions from classmates like, "What did you get for Christmas?" He explained that they didn't really care what we got; it was just a leading question so they could tell us what *they* got.

So, we would say, "Oh, socks and stuff," and ask what they got; problem averted. It was painfully obvious that we didn't fit in. Of course, once we moved into one house and went to school with the Jeffs, lying was unnecessary. It was just plain denial.

As one of thirty-one children in one household, (which was eventually more like twenty-four because the older siblings had married and moved out), I felt like a number. I was just another mouth to feed, another child to manage with chores. I sensed this in my interactions with others and—well, in everything. We were expected to be *perfect.* It's what our doctrine taught, what our parents and elders pretended to be, and, frankly, the only way to get to Heaven. As a young, virile man, I felt dirty and unworthy, and I had no idea the level of deception and hypocrisy the grownups were operating in.

The weight was unbearable at times. We had to go into Father's den each Sunday before bedtime and tell him how many times we had masturbated that week. My dad could have multiple sex partners—oh, I mean wives—but I had to fight the raging hormones in my body; it just wasn't fair. There were many times I considered driving at top speed right into a concrete freeway support. *Why not end it all? I'm going to burn in hell anyway; may as well get it started.* The level of humiliation, and then the guilt from eventually lying to my father to get his approval, was numbing my soul. I was going through the motions, smiling and upholding the family mantra of "keeping sweet" until I just wanted to throw up.

I thought I just needed to understand better, so I studied and studied the books available to me, the ones with all the dust on them that no one else read. Time after time, I would stumble across contradictions in what one apostle would say versus another. I would go to my father with these deep profound questions, and every time he would tell me not to worry myself about it.

"Son, when you've received more light and knowledge, you'll understand," was his pat answer. I got so tired of hearing that, I could have screamed right then and there. But instead, I would bow my head and act like the dutiful son I was supposed to be. More stuffing of my feelings, more faking it every day. God, it got lonely.

———

Our house, when we finally all moved in together after living in several different households, was a five thousand-square-foot home in Sandy. My father had found an apartment building that was being sold by the state so they could widen 33rd South Street. It was a twenty-three by one hundred and three-foot flat roof triplex unit with a minimum bid of two thousand dollars and a sealed bid process. My dad showed up with two envelope bids, one for the minimum and the other a competitive bid. No one else showed up so it was ours for two thousand dollars, and only eight years old at the time. It cost more to move it from 33rd South to 9730 South than it cost to buy it.

We placed the unit on top of a full basement, with a boys' dormitory on one end and a girls' dormitory on the other end. There were twenty-two bedrooms and eight bathrooms, two commercial water heaters, and two pairs of washers and dryers. Two of the living rooms in the original configuration were backed up to a common wall, which we removed. We then inserted a beam to span the length and gain the bearing load support lost. The dorm rooms were small, only seven by eleven feet—just enough room for a bed, dresser, and some space left over to do pushups, but at least it was my own room. Finally a little privacy.

The decibels at dinner time, however, were deafening. The other living room was turned into the large dining room, with a twenty-foot table that had benches on one side and chairs on the other. It was a big deal when I graduated from the bench to a chair. Here we learned that if we wanted second helpings, we had to eat fast!

My dad was a strong introvert and all the noise drove him crazy; he ate in his den. I don't think he liked little kids that much, and he considered you a little kid until you were out of high school. The boys did get one break from the chaos that consumed the dining room: once we had the priesthood, we didn't have to wash dishes anymore. That was a nice side benefit.

The priesthood is kind of weird in Mormonism. As young boys, you can receive the Aaronic Priesthood at the ripe young age of twelve with the title of "deacon," followed by "teacher," and then "priest." Once you hit eighteen, you can receive the Melchizedek Priesthood and become an "elder." The Aaronic Priesthood is the Levitical Priesthood from the line of Aaron, Moses' brother. The Melchizedek Priesthood comes from the Old Testament story of Abraham tithing to Melchizedek and was supposedly the priesthood that Jesus gave to Joseph Smith. (I know, it's confusing; sorry.)

For us Mackert boys, we were just thrilled to not have to wash dishes any more.

———

All my older brothers went straight to Short Creek, now Colorado City, to serve their two-year mission once they graduated. I was excused from this requirement. While I was in high school, I received some advanced training from the local Ford training center. One student from each high school auto program in the district was selected to attend three and a half hours of extra training two nights a week for thirty weeks. That was 2,100 extra hours of advanced training.

Because I applied myself in the program, both my instructor at the high school and my instructor from the

Ford training center recommended that I not attend a vocational training school. One said I would learn more in two weeks on the job than two more years in school! I was hired immediately by the local Chevy and Oldsmobile dealer, which allowed me to stay home—and give my paycheck to my father each week.

Once I graduated from high school, my father treated me completely differently. I remember going out for a steak dinner, just he and I, to celebrate my graduation. It was the first time I had eaten at a restaurant. The waitress asked if he wanted any A-1 sauce for his steak and he gruffly responded, "Why, is there something wrong with the steak?" I've never put anything on a steak to this day.

My dad took up bowling later in life and got really good at it. We boys played around at it, but it was mostly an excuse to drink and goof around. Once I graduated, my dad invited me to bowl with him in a league and eventually in tournaments. That was when he first bought me a beer. I wasn't even twenty-one, but had a dark and heavy beard so I was seldom asked for ID.

This was a really strange time for me, I didn't know how to react to my dad suddenly treating me like an equal when up until that point he had barely acknowledged me at all.

CHAPTER THREE

Life in a Three-Mother Household

I've been asked by several people if I've watched the HBO series *Sister Wives*. My response in usually, "No, I lived that. Why relive the pain?"

I've heard the consultant for the program was ex-FLDS. I'm not sure what they came up with from their experience, but for me, the underlying tension in the home between the wives—although undefined and never discussed—was definitely palpable. Many times that tension was taken out on us children, with spankings that exceeded the infraction. We felt like we were walking on eggshells at times, just trying to "lay low and let the storm pass."

I was always very close to my own mother, though. Born Mildred Edna Eads in Flagler, Colorado on May

14th, 1922, she was one of nine children of Lon and Lucy Eads. The family had a farm with milk cows and a large garden, which sustained them through the Great Depression. Like many of her generation, my mother's experiences in the Depression marked her for life, and we children could never get her to throw anything away. We would get the girls to take her somewhere and the boys would clean out the storage room about once a year, most items going straight to the dump.

Mom—whom everyone called "Midge"—was a beautiful woman during her youth and, by her own account, was proposed to twenty-one times before she met my dad in 1943 at a bar in Denver. Clyde C. Mackert, a handsome soldier and a "very good dancer," literally swept her off her feet. They were married just over a month later. Mom told me later that his mother had insisted he take dancing lessons; boy am I glad he did.

Dad went back to Georgia until he got out of the Army, and Mom moved to Casper, Wyoming, where she gave birth to full-term twin girls. That's where she met Fawn Shapley Jessop, the woman from a polygamist Mormon community who converted her to Mormonism.

My dad was pressured into his conversion by my mother, as I mentioned earlier. He recounted later that he couldn't make any sense of it on his first attempt. Then one of the men in the group asked him if he had prayed. He told us children later that the only prayer he remembered was, "Now I lay me down to sleep." He prayed to be able to understand and when he opened up The Book of Mormon again, it was like a completely different book. He referred to that moment as his personal testimony.

Not long after my dad's conversion, he and my mom relocated to Short Creek, Arizona. No housing was available, which was when they cleaned out an old chicken coop and lived in it until something more suitable could be arranged (as if anything could be less suitable).

The Short Creek group (which converted my mother) also had a community in the Salt Lake City area and, during a trip there, my father met two sisters: Donna and Myra Kunz. Donna was an independent and intelligent young journalist with high aspirations. Her younger sister, Myra, was a buxom girl with beautiful, thick, dark hair. Donna admitted that she always believed my father only married her so he could then marry Myra, similar to the Rachel and Leah story from the Old Testament. In what I'm sure seemed like no time at all, my father had three wives and many small mouths to feed. To make ends meet, he taught at the school that was started up within the community to educate the many young minds. He and several other able-bodied men also worked during summers at the Kaibab Forest near the Grand Canyon, cutting down trees.

———

Their little community was more of a commune than anything else; they shared everything they had, and they all ate together "from the same pot of stew," as they said. Whatever needed to be done was done by someone, anyone, just to keep things rolling.

In 1953, the State of Arizona raided the towns and took the men to prison for "unlawful co-habitation," i.e., living with someone you're not married to. (Boy, would we solve the traffic problems in our large cities if we tried to enforce that one today.) The names and faces of the men were front-page news across the country, including in New York, where my grandparents lived. My grandfather Clyde sent a telegraph to my dad in the prison in Kingman, Arizona, offering to get him a good lawyer if he, my mom, and her children would move back to New York and live with them. My father refused and was disowned. I never met his parents. A year later, in 1954, *Life* magazine did a three-page article about my family, pictures and all. I was born in 1955, so was not included.

My father sired twenty-seven children, eleven of those by my mother: the twins; Carole and Constance, Lucy, Clyde (he was also a Clyde C., but with a different 'C' middle name than my father and grandfather), Philip, Paula (who was mentally impaired because of a one hundred and five-degree fever my mom had two weeks before delivery), Howard (that's me), Roberta, Stan, Andrea, and

Camille. My mom always wanted a dozen; she was so close. Her life really was all about raising her children. We all felt very close to her growing up.

Donna had nine children: Seth, Charlotte (who shared my birthday; I was three years younger), Shem, Karen, Stephen (the best natural athlete of us all), Ken, Mark, Maria, and Melanie (the baby of us all, and the sweetest). Myra had seven: Mary, Rowena, David, Kathleen, Paul, Laura, and Brian.

Besides Shem, David, and me (who were eleven days apart), there were other natural triplet groupings: Stan, Steve, and Paul; and Roberta, Karen, and Kathleen. We always had playmates, especially when we all moved into one house!

When my father died in 2002 at eighty-two years of age, he had two hundred and eighty-nine descendants: a hundred and eighty-nine from my mom and a hundred from the other two wives.[2]

———

At first, we lived in three homes—some purchased, others rented, and all spread out around the Salt Lake Valley. Dad would visit once every three days like clockwork.

---

2. For a chronology of my biological siblings, see the Appendix at the end of this book.

But during the week, we would usually be asleep before he got home and still sleeping when he would leave for work. This was normal unless we had to stay up until he got home for some extra discipline, which I seldom did. We saw him on Sundays for our gathered family Sunday school teaching times. He would teach us from the early Mormon teachings, the fundamentals, church history, or the life of Joseph Smith.

We all learned to recite that we believed that the Mormon Church was the true church and Joseph Smith was its prophet. The rest of us would go to the group meeting in the afternoon, but Father usually stayed home watching TV. We always referred to the other moms as Aunt Donna and Aunt Myra, until one of the apostles decided we should show more respect and only refer to our dad as Father and the other moms as Mother Donna and Mother Myra. That was weird, but we adapted.

Mother Donna always seemed to have the house in the country that had acreage and room for a big garden. Many of my younger summers were spent living at Mother Donna's farm. Shem was the ringleader of our triplet group since it was his house. They would often board horses and Shem was an amazing horseman; I, on the other hand, barely survived it. Mother Donna was a very strict disciplinarian and often claimed to be able to discern when a child was lying. If you got in trouble and she suspected you were lying about it, her harsh punishments were very effective at coaxing out a confession. We feared Mother Donna more than Father.

I often felt singled out at times and didn't understand why. Looking back, it might be fair to assume it was because I was the legal wife's child. I'll never forget swearing at Shem, calling him a bastard, not even knowing what it meant. But he knew and beat the living crap out of me. I guess the lack of harmony ran deeper than the children were aware. We were not even teens, so someone must have explained it to him.

Mother Donna was also an herbal wizard. She had a miracle tea for everything from a nosebleed to migraine headaches. Most of her concoctions tasted horrible. We kids would rather have had the malady than the cure!

One year, after we were in the big house, she went to some health convention and came back convinced we needed cod liver oil every day. She had a mint-flavored mixture that was supposed to make it more tolerable, but it still gave us fish oil burps all day long. She thought if she mixed it with milk, it would be better. She would come down the hall of the boys' dorm, shaking the containers to mix the oil with the milk. If we heard her in time, we would bolt to the bathroom and act preoccupied. Otherwise, we had to drink it in front of her, no cheating. If we made it to the bathroom, she would leave it at the door. Then when she was gone, we would pour it down the drain and return the container when we went upstairs.

The large house in Sandy wasn't our first effort at living under one roof. I was in the eighth grade when we rented the large house up on the Avenues in Salt Lake City, just north of the Temple. It had four floors and was built on a steep road, so the main floor and basement both had street access. We commuted to Sandy that year, until our large house could be completed. That was the first time we all lived together under one roof.

We didn't have a lot of interaction with the other mothers before we all moved into one house, except for the boys' summer visits to care for the garden and animals. I was young and preoccupied with surviving and getting enough attention to do so, which was probably why I didn't notice any of the subtle interactions between the women. I do know there was a definite "pecking order" between the children, with Myra's children usually ending up last. I've spoken to many women who couldn't imagine sharing their husband with another woman, much less their sister. Talk about a sibling rivalry!

Like other dutiful religious people, the mothers tried their best to hide their conflicts from the children. I can only imagine the issues my father had to mediate. I remember a time when I was fifteen or sixteen and Mother Myra tried to beat me with a broom, but I just took it away from her. Of course, I was called into Father's den. He told her if I was big enough to take the broom away, I was probably too big to spank. He then asked if

I had any idea the grief it caused him when I did things like that. I tried hard not to make his life any tougher from then on.

———

The mothers would take turns with the areas of need in running the house: cooking, cleaning, and caring for young children. They would rotate whose girls worked with which mother, to avoid favoritism. The boys had their chores as well: yard work—like planting, weeding, and harvesting the garden—and caring for the animals. Whoever was responsible for feeding the tribe for the week would get an allowance, which was supposed to last all week.

My mom often bragged that she was the only one who would actually give money back to my dad at the end of the week instead of asking for more. She was very frugal indeed. She would go to the local grocery store and make a deal with the produce manager to put the spoiled fruit—the produce with bad spots they couldn't sell—into a box for her to pick up every second or third day. That way, we simply cut off the bad spots and had ripe fruit year round.

She also bought wheat in one hundred-pound bags, ground the wheat into flour, and baked homemade bread. When she did, it was time to clean out the leftovers from the fridge. Everything went into the blender and then into the bread dough. It made the most amazingly dense, hearty, whole wheat bread you've ever tasted, but once in a while you would see a few broccoli specs in it!

Mom would also go to the local fruit orchards and talk the owners into letting us glean the trees. The professional pickers would get the easy stuff and move on, but we little kids could climb high and reach those left behind. Some of my earliest memories are of climbing those trees. We found out quickly that apricot limbs don't hold much weight at all; luckily no one broke any bones in the process. As we got older, we would work in the orchards and get paid in fruit. Everything we picked was bottled and put in our fruit cellars for winter.

We would also can green beans, tomatoes, and every kind of fruit we could get. Our favorite summer meal was peaches with Mom's bread and peanut butter. We always ran out of peaches before the next crop came on. My mom got tired of us complaining, so one year we picked and bottled thirty bushel of peaches! That year we barely made it to the next crop. But for all her frugalness, her children never got anything extra like some of the other kids. It was more important to her to give a little back to my dad than to buy something special for any of us.

Later in life, in a guided meditation, I recalled the only Christmas I could remember. We popped popcorn, put together a jigsaw puzzle, played games, and even sat while Lucy read us a story. But the best part was that there were no chores; it was like an extra Sunday. I was asked if I received any gifts, but I couldn't recall a one. I really wanted a big yellow Tonka Truck, big enough to put my knee on its bed and propel myself with the other leg, like rowing a boat. As I pondered the scene further, I realized a toy like that would have made me feel significant.

That's what I lacked—significance. At times it felt like I was just a number, nothing special. "Don't make a scene and keep sweet," my father continually told us. So I did.

CHAPTER FOUR

Childhood Memories

Our big house was on six and a half acres with a small run-down barn and large fields to the north and south. The acreage south of us had a herd of Black Angus, and the bulls were particularly mean.

For sport, we would climb through the barbed wire fence and run around among the cows until a bull noticed us. Then we would sprint as fast as we could to get back on our safe side of the barbs. Many times someone would have to hold open the gap between the barbed wires to give room to dive through, just in front of the angry bull. It was a game to see who could get closest to disaster.

Every year, we bought a young bull of our own, which had to be grain fed for slaughter that fall. We would also buy a "dogie lamb," which is a twin that has been rejected by its mother. These lambs were very young and required bottle feeding by hand. As they got older, you had to be very careful or they would head butt you in an unpleasant place. The lamb would also be slaughtered for its meat in the fall.

Invariably, the girls would name all the animals, which made it difficult for them to eat the meat that fall and winter. If the boys wanted a larger helping, all we had to do was say the name of whichever animal was being served for dinner, and remark how tasty it was. That would send the girls off in tears, leaving more for us.

One year, we got a milk cow and a heifer instead of a bull. They were a lot more work, and since we had to milk Rosie through the winter, the barn had to be repaired and made more weather tight. At 6:00 each morning and night, Rosie got milked. At first, we three boys took turns, but when Shem and Dave graduated and went on their mission to Colorado City, I was left with the milking duties.

My senior year of high school was spent milking Rosie. She was a Guernsey cow, pretty brown with white spots, and she would give us between two and two and a half gallons per milking, and 50 percent cream. We had more cream than we knew what to do with! We would fill a two-quart jar and shake it until it turned to butter. Mom would make cottage cheese to help use it up. I still don't like drinking milk to this day; it completely ruined milk for me. Somehow the smell of the barn is still associated with the smell and taste of milk, yuck.

Each fall we would have the cows bred. It was timed for a spring delivery, so the little one didn't have to deal with the snow. We couldn't wait for the time we stopped milking Rosie so she could have milk for the calf. Once the calf was weaned, we had to start milking again. The heifer would also be bred, and invariably one of the two would have a bull calf, giving us meat for the upcoming winter.

———

Some of the mothers in our household could sew clothes and eventually the older girls learned how as well. Homemade, hand-me-down clothes were the norm; however, my older brother Phil had a year where he didn't grow much, so I handed some things "up" to him as I outgrew them. In the fourth grade, I forgot when the school pictures were going to be taken and wore a handmade hand-me-down shirt, preserved forever in that picture.

Until my sisters were old enough to babysit, the mother who had borne the latest child would get to stay home and care for the other little ones. The other mothers would work. Mother Myra managed a doctor's office; Mother Donna worked at a local newspaper. My mom worked on an assembly line eight hours a day, standing on concrete. Everyone contributed to help make ends meet. My father was a CPA, so that helped a lot, but he hadn't disclosed his felony record for polygamy, on his application, so we had to do everything we could to not draw any attention to ourselves.

When the children were old enough, we did whatever we could to work and bring in extra income. Besides orchards, we had paper routes—which meant 4:00 am wake ups to help fold papers and wrap a rubber band around them for delivery. We rode the darkened early morning streets on our bikes, throwing papers onto the front steps of houses while on the move. We would make it a game; after all, we competed in everything. On particularly blustery days, my mom would drive us on our routes. Now that I think about it, that job was great training for throwing water balloons and snowballs. We developed deadly aim!

Since my two-days-younger brother Shem lived on a farm in the Salt Lake Valley before we all moved in together, we often stayed at the farm and cared for the pasture. By and large, the biggest responsibility (which took the greatest amount of work) was the irrigation preparation and maintenance. There was no sprinkler system at the farm. So, completely "by hand," we had to arrange a flow of water through a network of canals and ditches, carefully making sure that water flooded every area of the three-acre farm. We had to go to the head (source) of the flow, and change the boards in the head-gates in order to redirect the water.

The most interesting part of irrigation maintenance chores was that we had approximately five days and four hours between each one of our shifts. This meant that often, our shift would happen in the middle of the night. Naturally, the middle of the night was the perfect time to have a little fun.

There was a rancher in our area who had some young calves we brothers loved to ride. We'd hop on their backs and hold on for dear life as they kicked and bucked with all of their strength. We'd hoot and holler and egg each other on. However, over time, the calves got used to our riding, and they eventually calmed down each time we hopped on board. We learned to yank their tails just enough to make them angry and begin bucking again. Other times, we'd play in the neighboring farmer's wheat field. The wheat would get so tall we could tunnel around in it, playing hide and seek by nothing but the light of the moon.

One day, somehow, Shem got his hands on a Welsh pony named Cinnamon. Boy, was she fast. With Shem on her back, she'd fly like the wind. Confident in her abilities, he was always trying to race any horse within a few miles of us. The two of them had quite the reputation.

Once, he even beat a thoroughbred on a nearby farm! I, on the other hand, was never comfortable on a horse.

That didn't stop me, however, from hopping on a horse when I thought it served my best interests—like impressing a girl. When I was in early high school, I had a crush on a sweet girl named Becky Fisher (who later went on to marry Shem in a prearranged marriage). She lived in Colorado City and owned a beautiful and spirited buckskin stallion named Shadow. One summer, Shem, Dave, and I decided to ride horses out to "The Gap," a local landmark. I borrowed Shadow, thinking it was a surefire way to make an impression on Becky. Spoiler alert: I was wrong.

Once we were ready to head out, Shem thought it would be funny to make Shadow take off with me on his back. Being a stallion, he always had to be in the lead, so Shem would nudge his nag a head in front and Shadow would break into an all-out sprint, with me hanging on, maybe screaming a little. One of my brothers thought it would be a great idea to give Shadow a little nudge on the hip. Just as my brother suspected, he bolted off, leaving everyone else in his dust. No matter what I did (kick, pull, shout), he wouldn't slow down. It was all I could do to keep hold of the reins and keep my rear end from flying out of the saddle. By the time my brothers caught up to me, they were laughing so hard they nearly fell off their horses!

While horses were easy to come by in our rural area, dogs, weren't as common as you'd think. To my very frugal mother, dogs were just another mouth to feed. I begged for a dog, year after year, but was never allowed one. Shem's older brother, Seth, though, had a little dog named Ginger. She was the coolest, smartest, and most fiercely loyal dog I'd ever known. She would chase dogs four times her size off the property, and had a growl so intimidating they would surely never come back. I loved that dog like she was my own.

You might say I had a very conservative, values-based upbringing as a child, despite its other peculiarities. Honesty, frugality, and hard work were not only emphasized—they were required.

Because there was never extra money to spend, we didn't get an allowance and we never received or gave gifts. My mom or older sister packed every single one of us a sack lunch every day, along with a single dime to pay for a carton of milk for each day of the week. Every Monday morning I went straight to the vending machine and bought a Creamsicle. Having spending money was a foreign concept to me. That dime a week was a rare privilege.

One day, when I was in the fifth or sixth grade, I was walking home from school and stopped with some friends at a 7-Eleven store so they could buy some candy. Of course, I had empty pockets, so I just stood back and waited. While inside, I noticed a penny candy lying on the floor. I went over my options internally, and rationalized that the employees would eventually just sweep it up and throw it out. No one would be the wiser if I took it! I scooped it up and shoved it in my pocket. But for weeks, my conscience drove me crazy.

After days of not even being able to sleep at night because of my guilt, I approached my mom and told her about what I had done. "Do you know what the Bible says about stealing?" she asked me sternly. I told her I didn't. "If you steal, you must pay it back seven times," she said. Naturally, my punishment was to earn seven cents in order to pay back that penny candy.

I washed the windows inside and out on our two-story house for one penny.

I scrubbed and waxed the entire kitchen floor for another penny.

I mowed the lawn, front and back, for the next.

I shoveled snow off our driveway and the neighbors' driveway in order to earn the rest.

Once I had all seven cents, my mom escorted me back to the 7-Eleven. As we entered, I had tears of embarrassment running down my very warm, very flushed cheeks. I shoved all of my pennies across the counter to the cashier who was working there. Do you know what he did? He just pushed them back toward me. "It's okay," he said. "It's no big deal. You keep it."

With that, my mom slammed her fist down on the counter so hard the change must have jumped six inches in the air. "NO!' she insisted loudly. "He needs to learn there are consequences for his actions. Don't you think he should learn from his mistakes?" she demanded, her voice slightly raised. "Don't you think he needs to learn a lesson about natural consequences? Please! Take his money!"

We walked outside, leaving the pennies behind. As hard and embarrassing as that was, I felt lighter on my feet walking home that day. I knew my mom cared about my character. For a kid who usually felt like a number, that actually felt good. What I did—and why I did it— mattered, at least to her.

———

That being said, in the bigger picture, the religious pressure for perfection in our home and community was overpowering. Complaining was not allowed; you just stuffed it down and moved on, fake smiles and all. Every morning, we would gather for family prayer and read my dad's daily commands; the most important was, as I mentioned, to "keep a sweet spirit at all times." If it were someone's birthday that day, we would sing to them and then on Sunday. If your birthday was that week, there might be some candles in a cake. No presents, nothing special—another reason to simply feel like a number. Just call me number three of four, or seven of eleven. I was my mom's third of four boys and seventh child.

My mom often told me that Mother Donna had more faith in her little finger than my mom had in her whole body. I think that was part of the religious pecking order; the convert family members were made to feel inferior to the blue bloods.

CHAPTER FIVE

A 25-Year-Old
Divorced Virgin

Because of the pre-arranged marriage system in the FLDS (a "revelation from God" about whom you're supposed to marry), there wasn't much interaction allowed between boys and girls in our community. The only form of contact allowed was the monthly square dance at the town hall in Colorado City. These were left-overs from the courtship days of my parents, and we had to travel three hundred and fifty miles from Salt Lake City to get there. It was worth it; that was literally the only time we were permitted to touch a girl, albeit only on one hand and her waist.

Some of us became pretty good dancers and, of course, there were some beautiful girls at these gatherings (even if they were dressed a hundred years behind the times). The girls wore no makeup and their hair was always pulled back from their faces. Nothing was allowed to make them more "seductive." They wore dresses that went to mid-calf at the highest and had long sleeves, just like the boys' shirts.

Even so, it was crazy how exhilarating the touch of a hand could be when we were so restricted. Of course, these events were thoroughly chaperoned by adults, some who would put on quite a display of refined dancing. But since the dances were always in Colorado City, we northern boys were at a distinct disadvantage when we did attend, as we didn't quite have the same skills.

Early one Sunday morning, shortly before I left for college, I received an unexpected phone call. It was the "prophet" of our group, Leroy (Roy) Johnson, or "Uncle Roy," as he was called. He asked me if I knew _____. He hesitated before coming up with the name, and asked to someone on the other end of the phone, "What's that girl's name?"

I heard my sister Carole's voice in the background, telling him a girl's name (my sister Carole was one of his wives). Uncle Roy proceeded to instruct me to meet the girl that afternoon and marry her the next day. Bizarrely, this was how all my older brothers and sisters had gotten married. The boys found out the day before and the girls got a week's notice.

Let me back up a little bit and set up the back story a bit more. My mom had twin girls, her first-born children. Constance, the oldest, known as Connie, married Bill, who was just a couple years older than she was; she had fifteen children. Her first six children were girls and she was a grandmother at thirty-six. Conversely, the other twin, Carole, married the prophet of the group, Roy Johnson. She was seventeen and he was seventy-two. There were no children from that marriage.

Now, when I heard Carole telling Uncle Roy (who technically, I suppose was my brother-in-law, not my uncle) the name of the girl I was supposed to marry, that was a red flag to me. You see, I knew the prophet was supposed to receive revelation *from God* who my wife was supposed to be, not from his own wife! What I was sure of, though, was that you always obeyed the prophet or else you were out.

The leaders in town were always looking for any reason to kick a young man out of the community, as it left more girls for them. There's actually a term for this: "culling the herd." So, a boy caught with a beer, or holding hands with a girl—or, God forbid, kissing a girl—would be subject to expulsion from the community. This produced a social sub-culture in Southern Utah called "the

Lost Boys," made up completely of FLDS boys, some as young as thirteen, who had been sent away.

To support the concept of pre-arranged marriages, they came up with a philosophy of "courtship after marriage." This meant you were supposed to keep yourself from any emotional attachment to the opposite sex until God revealed whom you were supposed to marry, and then instantly release your pent-up emotion in a "healthy" way. This was very destructive and many FLDS women reported being raped on their wedding night.

———

All of my older brothers and sisters married complete strangers except my brother Philip. He was just a bit older than me, with one sister between us. He was sweet on one of the Jeffs girls, but didn't tell anyone. She thought he was cute and to their surprise they were placed together and married in November of 1974.

My brother is an honorable man and took his time courting his new wife without forcing her too quickly. I had the honor of chauffeuring them on a delayed honeymoon between Christmas and New Year's. We took the week and drove to Southern California. I drove and they "got acquainted" in the back seat of a '69 Chevelle. I just adjusted my rear view mirror, averted my gaze, and minded my own business.

We stayed the first night with our Uncle Mel in Las Vegas, and the other nights in Vista, California with our Aunt Helen. We went to Disneyland, among other stops. I took some tools with me, which came in very handy when the car started to ping at low altitude. My brother always respected my mechanical abilities, and treated me with a bit of awe. His friendship is still one of my best and richest treasures.

———

But back to my own prospective bride. So, whom did they choose for *me*? At the time, I was twenty-four years old, five feet and eleven inches tall, a hundred and eighty-five pounds, and trying out for the college football team. I wanted to be a linebacker, then become a high school coach and a math teacher. My intended was seventeen and hadn't finished the eighth grade (she was taking correspondence courses and working to help support the family). Her dad had died in a trucking accident and she'd quit school to work full time and help support her mother, brothers, and sisters. Much to my dismay, it was far from love at first sight. To say she was heavier set than I was would be quite the understatement. And yet, the next day I married her!

You might wonder why the hell I would do that? The fact was, if I defied the prophet I would be out!

Excommunicated, a son of perdition, going to hell for certain. After twenty-four years of conditioning, I wasn't going to defy the prophet without some serious motivation. Besides, I knew plenty of larger women in our community (that being said, they'd had ten-plus kids, so they had a good reason). But many were some of my favorite people in the town. So I tried not to let her weight cloud my opinion.

And then there was my mom. Shortly after the call from the prophet, my mom called and said they had met the girl and she was very sweet, and above all, I needed to follow the prophet. I didn't want to disappoint my mother.

So, the next day, we went to the justice of the peace in St. George, Utah, where a judge performed the ceremony. He told me I could kiss the bride and I gave her a peck on the lips. He chuckled and said, "I bet you didn't win her with a kiss like that?" All I could think was, *I didn't win anything; this is the booby prize.*

I got married on Monday morning, June 2nd, 1980, and Monday night we had the religious ceremony that sealed us for "time and all eternity." This was an interesting event. Since the LDS temple ceremonies are secret, no one in the community really knew what happened there. It was a solemn event, and kind of disjointed. Perhaps this was because some of the temple details had been passed down by old timers whose memory was a bit suspect. This was considered the most important of the wedding ceremonies, but was not legally binding because the prophet wasn't a licensed minister with any state. To this point, technically, my dad wasn't a polygamist because he only legally married my mom. The other three marriages were just private ceremonies performed by the prophet.

My parents were there and my mother was beaming from ear to ear. She just wanted to get me in tight with the prophet. She'd always had great hopes of me going far, climbing the ladder, and being somebody important within the community.

My new wife was young and afraid of sex and, honestly, I wasn't motivated. Because of that, we never consummated the marriage. Our marriage wasn't easy on a number of levels, but most distressing to me was her lack of education. She was constantly stopping me to ask what a word meant. She had some serious emotional issues and, of course, along with those were the corresponding health issues. She got a job at a nursing home owned by one of the community members, but missed more work than she actually performed. I was employed at a GM dealership during those days, and working out in the evenings preparing for football tryouts.

I rented a place across the street from my brother Phil, his wife, and their three children, including a boy who looked just like me at his age and a little girl, April who absolutely stole my heart. She was the cutest, sweetest little thing I'd ever seen (and, trust me, I'd seen a lot of babies in my short life up till then). When April would cuddle up on my lap, my heart melted.

So, here I had my brother's family across the street, living a life that starkly contrasted with mine. I was married to a complete stranger who didn't interest me at all. But I was being faithful and obedient, even though there was no life or love in it.

———

I worked at the GM dealership for six years after graduating from high school and before I decided to go to college. One of my HS teachers was also employed there in the summers, and every year he would ask me why I was still there, why I hadn't gone to college. Obviously, with twenty-seven children, my dad wouldn't be paying for anything! Frankly, I hadn't even considered the possibility.

But one day, one of the older mechanics, a few years from retiring, walked up to the office, his face white as a sheet, and fell down in a dead faint right in front of me. The paramedics had to come and carry him out, and I truly thought I had just seen someone die. The man later recovered, but it highlighted the health hazards of my work environment. We had terrible exhaust fumes in the garage; the ventilation in the building was so bad that when we closed the doors for the winter, we would all get nosebleeds if we didn't put Vaseline in our noses.

I started to look around at the other workers in the building, imagining us all with one foot in the grave. College was suddenly looking pretty good!

I would be the first of my large family to attend a four-year university, but school had always been a place where I thrived I loved learning, especially math, and had graduated in the top three percent of my class in high school. I never skipped even one class. Considering my own mortality only served to remind me how much I enjoyed being in school.

———

At this point, I was realizing that "courtship after marriage" wasn't working for me. But was I ready to jettison everything I'd believed my whole life? Not quite yet. "Conflicted" is a mild way to describe my life at that time.

A few months later, just after starting college that fall, I woke up one morning and the thought struck me, *Oh my God, with my luck, the first time we do "it," she will get pregnant and I'll be stuck.* I couldn't imagine walking away from my own child, and the courts never gave custody to men back then. Recalling that moment, it seems the word "stuck" echoed in my head. It was like somebody threw a cold bucket of water on me and I woke up.

I thought, *What the heck am I doing? This is ridiculous!* Giving control of my life to somebody who was pretending that he'd heard from God about me was simply playing a sick game.

So, I sent my "wife" back home. I told her, "I'm sorry, I don't love you; I tried to and I don't. Go home; they'll give you to somebody who can love you and you'll be happier."

It didn't take long for the phone to start ringing.

They told me to just take her back; they would say nothing and within a year they would give me somebody that I could love.

I said, "No way; life is way too short to be in a situation like that."

Next they told me I was the only one strong enough to handle her emotional problems.

I told them, in no uncertain terms, that dog didn't hunt!

My sister Carole told me she was just the kind of girl I needed; if I'd take her everywhere I went, I wouldn't get in trouble. (You're right, Carole, because I wouldn't leave the house!)

That may sound a little harsh, but I was a twenty-four-year-old kid who had been controlled my whole life, and I was *done*. My poor mom cried for three days; she'd had such high hopes for me, and she really believed in the prophet.

So, there I was, nearly twenty-five years old, divorced, and still a virgin. Now I was on my own and making all my decisions myself (kind of an odd but freeing sensation). I had always been an outwardly confident individual, despite my insecurities, and suddenly found myself set free in a world that was far from the religious one to which I'd been accustomed.

I rented an apartment for a short while with my friend Mitch. I was named after his dad, who had been close to my family when he was young and my parents lived in town. That Howard, who was named for Mitch's father, the old Howard, was a different person. Now, here in Cedar Utah, attending Southern Utah State College, I was getting to know a whole new Howard—a whole new me.

Mitch would tell me of the false rumors that were spreading about me around town. They couldn't stand for anyone to deny the prophet and taught that once you turned your back on their truth, you would go into deep darkness. But it didn't feel like deep darkness to me. I was enjoying freedom from control and manipulation for the first time in my life and I liked it. I liked it a lot!

I don't recall when Mitch and I stopped being roommates, but since I had a good paying job as a mechanic at the GM dealership, I could soon afford to share a house on campus with a few other men. That was when I met two brothers, Jeff and Danny. Jeff was going to college on the GI Bill; he had been in the Navy, stationed in the

Bahamas. Danny was pre-med, training to be a chiropractor. Danny was the only contact in town for the best Humbolt County weed, known as stink weed.

At our place, we threw the best parties on campus, with the highest girl-to-guy ratios. This was a time when I experimented with most of the things that had been denied in my life up until then. I tried to play it somewhat safe; I never stuck a needle in my arm or took anything that would cause flash backs. I also didn't party during the week; I knew I needed my focus for classes and work. I scheduled all my classes in the morning and worked at the GM dealership in the afternoons. That was a great set up; the dealer was busiest in the summer when I was out of school, so I worked hard to minimize the student loans.

I nearly enlisted in the Navy as a nuclear propulsions officer. I found out about their program for college students who were in the sciences (math, chemistry, physics, etc.). They would pay me E3 wages for the last two years of my college and all I had to do was maintain a 3.0 GPA or better. I talked with a recruiting officer in Salt Lake City and sent him my transcripts. The only thing lacking was a year of physics and I was just finishing my spring quarter. That meant I had to complete a full year of physics in one quarter, on top of my other scheduled classes.

I went to the physics professor's room and was surprised to find my old high school calculus teacher, Mr. Smith. He remembered me, and after a few catch-up questions I explained my dilemma. He gave me an old copy of the textbook and explained that he would give me the midterm and finals, (no homework required) and I could work at my own pace. Boy, did that kill my social life for those months. I finished with a B average for fifteen credits and proudly walked into the recruiter's office that summer, ready to collect my extra pay.

In my mind, I was going to travel the world (a minimum of one year at sea was part of the program for the next four years, after eighteen months of extensive re-educating with a nuclear emphasis). It was a Saturday, and I hadn't shaved for a few days, which caught the recruiter off guard. He asked how old I was, which bothered me. We had gone over all that when I first inquired. Well, it turned out I was going to be six months too old to enter the program. He said I could go through the training and become an instructor in Florida. Yikes, I had never been east of the Rocky Mountains and didn't know then how much I would enjoy teaching. All that time spent studying physics wasted. I even had a new car all picked out and everything, dang it! So it was back to school and my math degree, along with statistics and computer science.

That junior year, I was offered an assistantship with Texas A&M for post-graduate work in statistics. That was miles away from sailing the seven seas, but was still long enough away from Southern Utah and the awkward moments when I would see a FLDS member in public and have to endure their elitist glances. I felt sorry for them. I had been set free from religious control and thought they might never know how good it felt. But still, I knew of my mom's disappointment, and that weighed on me.

CHAPTER SIX

Sports, Bloody Noses, and Longing

Between our work on the farms and our chores around the house, we kids contributed to running a household of dozens of people. Yet, we all still managed to find time for the sports we enjoyed.

I didn't necessarily love sports as much as most jocks, but I would do whatever it took to get attention and approval from my dad. He loved sports, so sports it was. I refused to let myself be just another number to him. I was going to be the son he was most proud of.

Dad had been a heavyweight boxer in college and in the Army. He told us he'd had a hundred and twenty-two amateur fights without a single loss. He was quick to add that he'd won many of his fights through a unique strategy his coach taught him. He would get up—no matter how tired he was—at the end of the three rounds, and he would dance around like he could go twelve more. No matter how beat down and exhausted he was, he would get up and act as if he were full of energy and piss and vinegar. He was convinced that this behavior—making his opponents believe he was far from tired—was what led to many victories or "draws."

My mom made him promise he would never teach us boys to fight. Even so, we always hade a couple pairs of boxing gloves lying around. With so many boys the same age, we had the perfect amount of "competition" for boxing practice. That being said, the fourteen-ounce gloves were more like having a pillow fight than a boxing match! We also had a pair of twelve-ounce gloves for the bigger boys to pummel each other with (for context, the pros use ten-ounce gloves). Even if we didn't know or acknowledge it at the time, our eagerness to learn to box came directly from our shared desire to have just one meaningful, physical interaction with our dad.

As brothers often do, we would have arguments. Our preferred way of settling them was with the gloves. Our older brothers would "glove us up" as early as five years old! Shem was the giant of the group—he was always a half head taller than David and me, and he had hands and arms twice as big as ours. When we tried to settle things, he would hit my face and nose while I just swung at the air, never making contact. But don't feel sorry for me, I eventually got my payback.

It was years later, when I was in college, that one of the football coaches I'd gotten to know during my attempt to make the team informed me he was putting together a night of boxing for the student body. He knew I was around a hundred and eighty-five pounds and asked if I'd fight a local sixteen-year-old farm kid who was undefeated at the time. I don't think he knew of my boxing history; he just needed a warm body to sacrifice to the "boxing gods." I was excited for the opportunity to actually fight in a ring instead of just my backyard. I instantly changed my workout routine to include time on the speed and heavy bags. I even did some shadow boxing while I ran for endurance training.

About a week before the match, I challenged Shem to spar with me. At that time, I could bench press two hundred and eighty-five pounds, free bar. I was the strongest I had ever been in my life. After a few fast and well placed jabs and a stout left hook, Shem stepped back, a hint of blood (or, as I like to think, a hint of humiliation), at the edge of his nostril, and declared that I had never hit him like that before! My long-awaited revenge had been served up a decade later, but it was still sweet.

When the "night at the fights" arrived, it was finally time to fight the opponent I had been recruited to face. I gave the kid a great fight, but late in the last round I had him on the ropes and just couldn't punch through his defenses. That was when I made the rookie mistake and reared back with what we called a "cowboy punch." That left my chin wide open to attack and he sprang off the ropes and dropped me like a bad habit.

My brother Seth was there and came up to me afterwards, laughing. I had stood before the ten count, but when the ref grabbed my hands and shook my arms, Seth said I looked like Gumby, wobbly as rubber. I had not prevailed, but I was completely satisfied; I had secured my own prize!

I continued boxing here and there all the way through college. Inwardly, I was hoping my father would be gratified at my efforts in the sport. I fought one more time in a college-sponsored fight and won, but then in November of 1982, the lightweight boxing champion of the world, Boom Boom Mancini, killed the Korean boxer Duk Koo Kim in a sanctioned fight. This tragic event showed what can happen when you get knocked out, and this ended my boxing experiment for good. I figured I needed my grey matter for my studies.

———

My dad was a big guy—six feet tall and two hundred pounds when he was fifteen years old. He played center and middle linebacker for his high school football team. Back then, no quarterbacks took the snap under center. Everything was "shotgun," and the center had to lead a running back precisely in order to make the play successful. To aid in his success, my grandfather attached a car tire to a rope and hung it from a tree branch. My dad would spend hours hiking the ball through the center of the swinging tire, the whole time keeping his head between his legs. He excelled at what he did.

One year, he broke his nose during a game and was fitted with one of the first face guards ever used in football. He ended up with four different colleges offering him full-ride scholarships. He decided to play for Syracuse, but mainly chose them because of their accounting program. It wasn't long after his freshman year started that he tried to join in the war effort. He approached the Marine Corps, the Air Force, and the Navy, but was turned away from all of them because of his poor eyesight. Finally, he walked into the Army recruiting office and realized the officer on duty was the father of one of his best friends in high school.

"Here's what you gotta do," the officer told him. "If you really want to serve your country—if you're bound and determined to make it happen—you've got to memorize that line on that eye chart poster right there." He said this as he was stepping out to get coffee, which gave my dad the chance to look over the poster and memorize it. Then, the recruiter stepped back in and gave Dad the test. He was in.

After boot camp, Dad was assigned to a paratrooper squad in Puerto Rico. He eventually became an MP (military police). As soon as the camp commander found out my dad was a good boxer, he made Dad their heavyweight fighter.

Boxing matches between forts were a huge morale booster in the military, and my father ended up being shipped all over to box heavyweight with fellow soldiers. Once the war was over, he went back to football and played semi-pro for the State of Utah. Along with boxing, his love for football translated into *our* love of football. I knew I'd do whatever it took to make sure my dad knew how worthy of his love I really was.

As soon as I could bend down without falling (around the age of two or three), I would hike the ball to my older brothers. Once Steve, Stan, or Paul could hike, I graduated to blocking and rushing. We all learned the correct techniques for all the positions and, eventually, my dad had enough sons to create an entire football team (with a few to spare!).

One Thanksgiving Day, the "triplets" decided to challenge the older brothers to a game of tackle football without any pads. Thanksgiving dinner wasn't going to be ready until 3:00, so we had time to use some of our pent-up energy. Four very long hours later, we were tied seventy-two to seventy-two (and not a single one of us could move the next day). This was the beginning of a decades-long tradition. Soon afterward, our sisters began getting married and we'd recruit their husbands to join in on the Turkey Day game.

Once, I had a perfect tackle on my half-sister's new husband, George. As I approached him, his eyes got as big as saucers. I pressed my head into his sternum, wrapped my arms around his legs, and drove him down into the ground. Within seconds, he had a broken sternum and I'd popped every single vertebra in my back. I kept playing, but did have to see a chiropractor the next day. George left and I don't think he ever played with us again. Of course, we did our best to suck it up and never let people in on the serious amount of pain we were in.

Though we all loved football, we were never allowed to play high school sports. Always hanging over our heads was the felony on Dad's record due to the FLDS compound raid in 1953. Because of this, he didn't want any attention drawn to our family name, and therefore any sport was absolutely out of the question. All the practice and experience we had was in our own yards or on the farm.

———

Despite the lack of exposure to organized sports, throughout my entire childhood and adolescence my dream was to play college football and then become a high school math teacher and football coach. I figured that even if I were a terrible coach, I would still have a job because math teachers were (and still are) in high demand. I decided to go to Southern Utah State College in Cedar City, Utah. It was small, so I had a better chance of making the team.

Walking onto a college campus and never having played high school football was a daunting prospect. They didn't have any film on me to evaluate my potential. I didn't have any sort of record or stats to speak of. I was a solid tackler and a very good pass defender, and I thought there would certainly be a spot for me. As I learned, I wasn't exactly big enough. *But of course I will be fast enough,* I thought.

But, it turned out that even the fastest Mackert boy wasn't fast enough for a college football team. After two weeks of practice, I found out I didn't make the travelling team. Just like that, my football experiment was over. For years after that, I still told people I played college ball, though, because my ego wouldn't let me admit my defeat. Not only was I trying to prove something to myself, but I was still trying to prove something to my dad.

When I didn't make the team, I hoped that if football wasn't my thing, he would still love me for my academic scholarship and my already well-paying job.

———

After my attempt at football didn't pan out, I started to rethink whether I wanted to be a teacher or not. Part of the motivation for my change of heart was my discovery that I could make twice the money after graduation with a straight math major. I had just missed the first quarter of calculus and didn't want to wait a year to start the scheduled path for graduation. Hoping I could somehow make it work, I met with the professor and talked him into letting me start in the winter quarter class (even though I missed the first). It took a little time but I soon caught up with everyone else.

I scheduled my classes for the mornings and continued to work at the GM dealership in the afternoons. In the summers, when the shop was the busiest and I was no longer in school, I would work as much as possible to set money aside for the winter.

Things were going well enough for me—I enjoyed my math major and statistics minor; work was busy and paid me enough to keep me afloat. But the August before my senior year, someone at Oldsmobile corporate reached out to interview me for a position as a District Service Manager in Billings, Montana. I was now faced with one of the biggest life decision I had to make to date. Should I finish my degree and pursue a masters degree in Stats at Texas A&M, then train to become an actuarial in the insurance field? This would be career math, which I was good at. But I would perhaps spend the rest of my life in a cubicle, talking to no one. (As an extrovert, this part didn't exactly excite me.)

Or, should I duck out of school and spend my time surrounded by the things I loved most—cars and people? It was only a matter of days before I had loaded up everything I owned and was heading to start my new life in Billings, Montana.

When I pulled into town, I didn't know a single person. I'd never even been to the state before! However, I had the phone number of one person, and that was the music pastor at Billings Bible Church.

As soon as I arrived, I called him, and was pleasantly surprised to find out he had arranged for me to move into the basement apartment of one of the church elders and his wife. When I got there, they had already cleared out the garage in order to make room for me to unload my stuff, unpack my boxes, and get settled. I could have been an axe-murderer or a total weirdo, but they trusted me and loved me already. This was my very first taste of Christian hospitality—and of real Christians.

Howard's mother,
Mildred Edna
Eads Mackert

Howard's three mothers

The Mackert family in the late 1960s

The Mackert boys, late 1960s

Howard with his sister Roberta

The infamous hand-me-down-shirt school photo

Howard (front row, third from left) and his brothers on the day of their father's funeral

"Midge's boys": Howard (second from left) with brothers Phil, Clyde, and Stan

Howard (right) and his brother Phil

The "triplets" at 60

Six generations

Howard and his mother

Howard and Rhonda on their wedding day

Howard and Rhonda Mackert today

CHAPTER SEVEN

Finding Jesus and Rhonda

You're probably wondering how I went from my exodus out of FLDS into a Christian church. To explain that, I need to back up a bit.

More than anything, I love to learn. In fact, every quarter of college, before I dropped out to move to Montana, I made the Dean's List honor roll. However, one quarter, I received my report card of straight A's only to find out that I was not on the list. *What? How was that possible?* I marched myself into the administrator's office with a head full of steam. Turns out, I only had fourteen credits, and you need a minimum of fifteen in order to make the Dean's List. I was going to make sure that never happened again.

I decided to fill my extra time slot (for extra credits) with one-on-one vocal lessons and a choir class at the university. I had been singing my whole life, and my mom always told me that I started whistling beautifully at only 18 months old. These were easy credits that added enjoyment and variety to my life.

One day, while sitting in choir, a cute blonde student walked in. She talked with the professor for a little while, and then bounced out. She was about five feet tall—just a tiny thing—with shiny, nearly white hair that trailed past her waist. Turned out she was the choreographer and music arranger for the professors' jazz ensemble. Her name was Heidi—Heidi from Appleton, Wisconsin. It wasn't long before I'd asked her out on a date.

Thanks to my job as a dealership technician, I had more disposable income than most of my college peers. I remember feeling on top of the world as we sat in a nice restaurant overlooking the valley, enjoying a couple of delicious steaks. Then, we were off to a local movie theater for a show, after which I drove her home. When we pulled up outside her dorm, before I could get the key out of the ignition, she turned to look at me, her eyes as big and as bright as ever.

"How do you feel about Jesus?" she asked me directly. That was certainly the last thing on my mind.

"Well, what do you mean?" I stammered. "I mean, I believe he died on the cross and all that."

"Yes," she said, "but I mean, how do you feel about him as your personal Lord and Savior?"

I was a bit befuddled. Even though I'd left the FLDS and the Mormon faith, I still believed somewhere in the back of my mind that the Mormon god was up in heaven, creating spirit bodies for the next planet he might create. Jesus as my personal Lord and Savior? The thought had never occurred to me. I didn't even know what that meant.

———

The conversation between us went on quite passionately as we got to discussing creationism versus evolution. As a scientist and mathematician, evolution was a fact to me, not a theory. We went inside, where we talked and argued until 3:00 a.m.

In her frustration with my reluctance to accept her truth, she handed me a book—the Bible. "Do you believe the Bible is true?" she asked me. I had to admit I'd never read more than the book of Matthew.

On top of the Bible, she placed a little pamphlet called "To Moroni with Love." (Moroni is the angel on top of all the Mormon temples, who is believed to have given the golden plates to Joseph Smith, which Joseph Smith then translated into the Book of Mormon). "To Moroni with Love" was written by Ed Decker with an organization called Ex-Mormons for Jesus, and it started with an odd statement: that in writing it, Decker hoped for one of two results. He hoped that it would either make the reader a stronger Mormon (not what I was expecting), or that it would cause him/her to question Mormonism's beliefs—his hope being the reader would look for answers in the Bible.

The next day, I opened it up and read with interest. It started out with quotes from the Mormon books I was trained in. These were followed by statements from the Bible that directly contradicted those Mormon teachings. I was stunned.

In the FLDS, one of the requirements for getting the priesthood was that we memorize the "Articles of Faith." One of them states "We believe the Bible to be the word of God as far as it is translated correctly. We also believe the Book of Mormon to be the word of God." I worked my way through the booklet, absolutely stunned to discover that the Bible so strongly contradicted Mormon teachings! This was the beginning of my re-programming.

I started going to church with Heidi, Ron (our music professor), and his wife, Christie. I was like a sponge, soaking up every ounce of information that I could. I was filled with questions, seeking and reading and inquiring every chance I could get.

But as intrigued and eager as I was, I still had a really big problem. I was deathly afraid that if I became a Christian—if I said "yes" to all of this—I would no longer have any fun. I figured that if God was as merciful as everyone said He was, maybe He'd give me a pat on the back for all the "good" that I did, and only a slap on the wrist for the times I was "bad." However, my time reading Scripture seemed to suggest otherwise.

—

One night, while reading the Gospel of Mark, I came across a Scripture passage in which a rich young ruler came to Jesus and called Him "good master."[3] Jesus corrected him and said that truly, no one is good except God. This stopped me in my tracks. If the only man to walk the earth without sin didn't call Himself good, how could I ever expect God to call me "good?"

In Sunday school, the pastor was teaching out of the book of Revelation and we were in the part about the tribulation. He was telling us about "the rapture," the belief that all Christians will be swept suddenly and mysteriously from the earth when Jesus returns, sparing them from a seven-year period of terrible persecution and affliction (i.e., "the tribulation"). The way he described it sounded awful, so I thought, *I'll just wait until right before the rapture to give my life to Jesus.* Unfortunately I'd studied logic in my college classes and recognized that if you don't know when something will happen, it's impossible to do something right before that.

---

3. See Luke 18.

Dang, I was still stuck and afraid I wouldn't have any fun if I became a Christian.

Now what do I do? I thought to myself. I was worried about fully committing to Christianity because the last thing I wanted was yet another lifestyle bound by rules and restrictions.

But pretty soon, I had another problem. I had heard about girls doing "evangelistic dating," and I suddenly got worried that Heidi was dating me only to recruit me to her side. Was our entire relationship a product of her attempt to turn an unbelieving man to the Lord?

Due to the norms of my upbringing, I always assumed that it was expected of me to marry Heidi (after all, I'd taken her out on dates, which of course meant that our wedding was imminent). However, I didn't feel romantically toward Heidi. She was a very sweet girl who was very important to me, but there wasn't a strong spark between us.

I went to Heidi with my concerns. Luckily, she assured me she wasn't "missionary dating" and we both agreed to start seeing other people. I breathed a sigh of relief. I was going to be a bachelor for some time longer.

Some time later, I was reading the Bible and came across a passage in the New Testament that stood out to me. The apostle Paul was talking about the human condition we all have—the things we really want to do, we don't do, and the things we don't want to do, we end up doing.[4] This was how I felt!

No matter how badly I wanted to do the right thing— that I didn't want to "sin"—I ended up making wrong choices. I was feeling remorseful and guilty for all the decisions I'd made that had been out of self-interest. I got on my knees and told God that I needed real, professional Help. I told Him I'd give my life to Him if He could help me make better decisions and be a more honorable man.

Almost instantly, I felt different. I suddenly stopped swearing and cursing, even though at the dealership I was known as the man with the mouth of a sailor. I felt at peace with the man in the mirror. Loving myself and not living with shame made me feel free—and I had a lot more fun! It turns out I didn't have any idea of what was truly fun after all. Liking the man in the mirror was definitely new to me.

Other things turned around too, almost immediately. Four days after I gave my life to God—the day I told Him I needed "professional help"—I received a call from the Oldsmobile Zone Service Manager from Denver. He wanted to hire me and move me to Montana. We interviewed each

---

4. See Romans 7.

other and both accepted, and I was off to Billings with everything I owned in the back of a Ryder truck.

At my job in Billings, I was the district service manager, which meant I had to sign every single Oldsmobile warranty claim in my district. I had to inspect the failed part, inspect the labor time charges, and give final approval. I was responsible for forty-eight dealerships in five states. That meant I spent a LOT of time in the car.

Wanting to grow in my new faith, I purchased the King James Bible on cassette tapes and listened to them over and over again while I drove. I had four loops: Loop One included Bozeman, Helena, and surrounding areas. Loop Two took me to Lewistown, Cut Bank, and Great Falls. Loop Three took me to Rapid City and Custer, South Dakota, and Cody Wyoming. Loop Four took me out to Nebraska, Colorado, and Southern Wyoming. I only spent one work day a week at home, which is when I worked at the dealership in Billings.

After six months in Billings, I was promoted to Denver, District One. In Montana, I called on one third of the dealerships but only 10 percent of the warranty volume. In Denver I had ten dealers and 30 percent of the volume. Now it was as if my yes to God opened all kinds of new doors, experiences, and favor. In my new position, I would spend only one night a month out of town. Being able to have a home base, so to speak, made me feel like I could at last settle down and really start my new life.

The first thing I needed to find was a church. I ended up at Mission Hills Baptist Church in Englewood, just south of Denver. There, the Pastor of Discipleship took me under his wing. I learned a lot about the Bible, about Jesus, and about life—and I really enjoyed strengthening my relationship with God as well as other like-minded people at the church.

However, I was still missing something. A relationship! A family! I felt like my life was racing past me. I joined the career singles group at the church, and we did all kinds of activities together. It was fun, but I still felt an emptiness. *I should have a family by now,* I thought to myself almost daily. I had visions of being sixty years old, trying to throw a football for my young son, and my arm falling off.

I brought my worries to one of the counseling pastors, and he said something to me I will never forget: "Don't marry the one you can live with, marry the one you can't live without!" This reminded me to keep my standards high and to not settle for the first lovely lady who walked into my life. Eventually, I became the president of the career singles group.

That summer, a local church was hosting a retreat over Labor Day Weekend. They were contracting with Tony Compolo to be the speaker—at that time, one of the biggest and most sought-after Christian speakers around. In an effort to be able to afford his price tag, that church opened up the retreat to all Denver-area churches. So, not only did I attend, but I was also invited to be on the planning committee. And that is how I ended up meeting Tamara, a close friend of my now-wife, Rhonda.

Rhonda would not have even been at the retreat if some guy hadn't paid for her registration. Truth be told, I was actually initially interested in someone else. And then I met Rhonda! At that point, Rhonda had been in a few relationships that didn't work out as planned, and in her words, "The last thing she was looking for at that retreat was a man." We seemed doomed to miss each other.

At the first meeting on Saturday, I was talking to Tamara, who was a fellow retreat board member. She introduced me to Rhonda, and I gave her a friendly hug. "You are exactly five-foot-three," I told her. "The exact same height as my mom," I added. (I know, not the smoothest of pick-up lines.) We chatted a little bit, and something about her lit a fire in me.

I was able to get her phone number from the retreat roster, and called her a couple days after the retreat was over. I asked her out for dinner (after reminding her who I was). She thought about it and said, "Sure!"

I was thirty years old at that time and Rhonda was twenty-four. I took her to a nice dinner for our first date, and as I walked into the restaurant, I knew she was the "one." Being with her felt like the fireworks I'd been look-ing for. I couldn't believe how gracious and caring God had been to me, answering my prayers just in the nick of time.

She, on the other hand, took some convincing.

———

I was reluctant to divulge the truth about my upbringing with Rhonda, in case it would scare her away. But after our first date, since I really thought she could be the one, I knew I didn't want to get very far down that road and then get rejected.

So, I sat her down and told her all about my family background. To her credit, she asked if I ever planned to go back. My emphatic response convinced her. And she, in return, told me that a man's past is just that, his past. I'm so grateful to this day that she was not weirded out by mine.

I thought I was getting old (thirty-one by this time), so we decided not to wait long to get married. To our delight, her parents quickly agreed to the courtship. When Rhonda's dad found out that I was a Christian AND a mechanic, he told her to marry me right away. For that, too, I am grateful. He was an amazing man. We set the wedding date for May 16th, only seven and a half months after we met.

CHAPTER EIGHT

Good Bye, Certainty

Learning to live as a Christian was a complete (well, almost complete) reprogramming of my spiritual understanding, with a few bumps along the way. For one, it took me from Mormon fundamentalism to . . . Christian fundamentalism. It was a case of out of the frying pan, into the fire.

I'd like to elaborate a bit on what I mean by fundamentalism. I'm talking about people who generally believe they are the *only* ones going to heaven. They have the corner on the truth, which to them is "absolute truth." They are in and you are out unless you believe exactly like they do.

Another identifier is the way they look down on people who are down and out. There is a perfectionism that is required, but which actually results in hypocrisy, and what is commonly known as "putting on one's Sunday best." This applies to how a person dresses, talks, acts and who they do those things with. (You may have heard the old quote, "We don't drink, smoke, or chew . . . or go out with those who do!") They insulate themselves from the dirty ones in the world for fear that "it" might rub off on them. Just picture the Pharisees of Jesus' time. He called them " white-washed tombs, full of all manner of wickedness." [5] You get the picture.

Note that this kind of attitude isn't particular to one denomination or sect or another. I experienced fundamentalism in both Mormon and Christian communities, and we all know it's in other religions as well. It's a worldview as much or more than a theology—one that is legalistic, separatist, and judgmental.

Another fatal flaw in fundamentalist thinking is the hair-splitting that goes on in these circles. Not only do you have to say the right words and follow the right motions, you have to read the "correct" translation of the Bible (usually the old King James Authorized Version. They seem to forget that the word "authorized" in the title doesn't mean God authorized it; the King of England authorized it!)

Yet another point to divide over, oddly enough, is one's interpretation of the most difficult and cryptic book in the Bible, the Book of Revelation. It never ends!

---

5. See Matthew 23:27-28

That is why there are nearly 10,000 different Protestant denominations to choose from—each with the "truth," many with no room for dissent to their core beliefs.

———

To be fair, when I younger and navigating the field of Christian beliefs, I genuinely had no reference points to measure what I was being told. At the time, I simply thought I was being taught the "right" way to believe, versus one of the other ways to believe. I was extremely impressed that people could and would study the original texts of the Bible, and that so many ancient manuscripts still existed.

This kind of scholarship was a stark contrast to the Mormonism I had known. Mormon leaders don't go to Bible school and study Greek and Hebrew. They are usually successful businessmen who have been major contributors of time and money. Most meetings are either faith-promoting stories or testimonies. So, this new level of depth intrigued me and I took it all in—"hook, line, and sinker"—and maybe even the whole boat and dock! I had no frame of reference for the principles and worldview being shared with me, and certainly had no idea of how they fit with the genesis of the Protestant denominations or even the historic changes within Catholicism. There was so much to learn.

In my early days after I left Mormonism, in Montana, I went to a conference on "inerrancy." (This is a doctrine that states that everything, every word written in the Bible, is true and without error in its original form.) The assumption of inerrancy, although not stated per se, is that God dictated what was to be written to all the authors of the books of the Bible—never mind the many books that were not included—in what is considered the Protestant Bible.

At first, I completely embraced this concept of absolute inerrancy. Since then, I've come to what I believe is a more well-rounded understanding of what "inspiration" means. In the New Testament Scriptures, both the apostles Paul and Peter state that "all Scripture is God-breathed" (another term for "inspired").[6] I don't think that means God grabbed the pen and personally wrote for the authors. "Inspired" has a more subtle meaning of influence, not control. I believe wholeheartedly that God used these men to communicate ideas and concepts that He placed in their hearts/minds. But I also believe they were unavoidably influenced by their own filters and history.

If you are familiar with the New Testament Book of Revelation, it might help to remember that it was written by Jesus' disciple John, one of the "Sons of Thunder" who asked Jesus if they should call down fire on that group

---

6. See 2 Timothy 3:16 and 2 Peter 1:20-21

that wasn't "with them."[7] I hardly think that thought was "God-breathed"!

The reality is that we can't help but filter our perception of God and what he is trying to tell us through our own life experiences and lessons. The apostle Paul said it this way: "We all look through a glass darkly,"[8] like a cloudy, unfiltered beer. We cannot see perfectly and so our conclusions are incomplete. Where the problem arises, in my opinion, is when we teach as if we are 100 percent certain.

When I look back on my years in FLDS, and then in Christian fundamentalism, I see some similarities—not in beliefs, but in attitude. How do well-meaning people get swallowed up in such rigidity? I truly believe it's partly because of their need for certainty—and their predisposition to gravitate to people and movements that appear to offer that assurance they have "ultimate truth."

Now, when I talk to someone who speaks rigidly with *certainty* about spiritual things, red warning lights go off and loud sirens in my head scream for me to pay attention and be cautious. I am convinced we all have a responsibility to be like the Bereans in the early Church, who, the Bible tells us, took the apostles' words into their

---

7. See Luke 9:54.
8. See 1 Corinthians 13:12, KJV.

hearts. They gave the message a chance, but searched the Scriptures to see if it was true.[9]

This has led me to believe that most of us "Christians" really need a "whole-gospel" perspective—dare I say a "whole-Bible" perspective? I think that, unless we realize that most truths in the Bible are held in tension with other truths, we can easily overemphasize on what we perceive to be "truth" and lose our balance. I've seen this over and over again.

For example: the "sovereignty versus free will" question is often raised in Christian circles. Does God control us, or do we have a choice in the matter? I would say "both/and." Both are true, and those truths must be held in tension with each other.

Another thing I was originally taught in the first churches I found myself in was that the miracles of Jesus' times have passed or been completed. In other words, God doesn't heal people anymore and speaking in tongues is of the devil. I really struggled with the healing thing as I read books from missionaries in Africa or other third-world areas. I found that, somehow, God could heal people over there, but not in America. *Huh?* I thought the Bible says God doesn't change.

It seemed the deeper I went into the stream of Christianity characterized by fundamentalism, the less I could

---

9. See Acts 17:11.

trust my emotions and my heart, and the more I relied on my logic—on things that were *certain.* Being a math major in college, I could track with this concrete way of thinking and I eagerly adopted those doctrines. I frequently lectured on Mormonism and loved authors like Walter Martin and his *Kingdom of the Cults.*

Looking back, I can say that no one is quite as passionate in working against cults as someone rescued from one. I'm sure there was a bit of that going on with me. The problem is that the cult can still be controlling you, your thoughts, and your energy by how much you're trying to push back against it.

I believe those who escape a cult should remove themselves as far as possible from them before going back to try and help. The apostle Paul said that he was "taken away" for thirteen or fourteen years for the repair of his understanding before beginning his ministry to the Gentiles. Even then, he didn't make the correcting of the Pharisees his focus, even though he was highly qualified to do so.

———

As time went on, I couldn't understand why our minds should be considered more trustworthy than our hearts. I suppose one reason we might trust our minds over our hearts is because they come up with some pretty convincing arguments that are difficult to refute. Logic and certainty can be very hard to argue. Feelings can be much more difficult to articulate and less convincing. Then, some argue that their mind has been renewed "by the washing of the Word," but what about the passages that talk about receiving a new heart, one that is tuned to God's frequency, His feelings and desires?

I remember hearing a fire-and-brimstone sermon about hell, and the speaker's summation of the counter-philosophy was that the other party had been "feminized" (i.e., trusting what feels good over what is right, as this is somehow a gender-specific thing?). Sadly, this speaker's "God" was obviously one that had to be appeased, feared, and avoided, one who would damn you to hell and not think twice, a God who created some for wrath and some for glory. That God didn't sound very approachable to me!

Many of those kinds of believers don't believe God is love, not really. They believe He is loving *when appropriate*. No, I believe, if God is really love, then we should be able to replace the word "love" in 1 Corinthians chapter 13 with the word "God." If we do, we read that God is longsuffering and keeps no record of wrongs.

Wait a minute, *really?*

I found that many of the Christians I was spending with at this time of my life had a "good cop, bad cop" version of the Trinity (the three persons of the Godhead—Father, Son, and Holy Spirit). They presented Jesus as the nice guy, but God the Father as the one who would whack you if you got out of line. *WOW.* I remember thinking, *If He truly removes our sins from us as far as the East is from the West, and keeps no record, then who will judge us?*

Jesus clearly states in John 5:22 that the Father doesn't judge anyone, but all judgment has been given to the Son. When the apostles asked to see the Father, Jesus responded with a bit of frustration, "How many years have you been with me? If you've seen me, you've seen the Father."[10] Evidently, Jesus is the one who will judge if any judgment is needed. He's also the one who rebuked the self-righteous spiritual leaders of His day, demanding that the one without sin should "cast the first stone"![11]

I was once told, with great certainty, that when Jesus cried out on the cross, accusing the Father of forsaking him, that it was because Jesus had "become sin for us" and had taken on the entirety of all the sins of all mankind, past, present, and future. Since God apparently cannot look upon sin with the least degree of allowance, He had to look away. *WOW* (again). What a cold-hearted analysis.

Once, around the Easter season, I was thinking about this scenario, and I felt God speaking to my spirit, saying that He had looked away because He couldn't stand to see His beloved son suffer any longer. It was too much for Him

---

10. See John 14:7.
11. See John 8.

to bear, which gives us some insight into how unbearable it must have been for Jesus. Is it any wonder that when the soldiers came to break his legs He was already dead?[12] Not to mention that He had been given thirty-nine lashes, which was enough to cause fatality on its own.

———

It was during these troubling times of doubt and theological suspicion that Rhonda and I were married. One thing that was quickly evident was that my logic might win me an argument, but it would not convince her I was right.

Early in our marriage, we took the Myers-Briggs personality test. I didn't score a single introverted point on the long test! I am an ESTJ: Extroverted-Sensing-Thinking-Judger. Rhonda, on the other hand, is an INFJ: Introverted-Intuitive-Feeling-Judger, and an outwardly skilled introvert. She can function as a pretend extrovert when the situation requires it. Mine is the most common personality type and hers' the rarest.

With my typical zeal, I dove into the system of categorizing people, animals, denominations, and anything else I could think of. Then as I studied about Rhonda's type—especially people who make decisions based on feelings—I was struck that her feelings made as much sense to her

---

12. See John 19:33.

as my logic did to me. Her method of decision-making took other people into account where mine was more about processes and outcomes.

I like to contrast those two types as leadership versus management. No one wants to be "managed," but we all want to be inspired to follow a dynamic leader. These observations and some significant epiphanies soon filtered into my theology. I thank God for Rhonda and her stubborn way of planting her feet and holding her ground until I began to see the value of her perspectives. She and God have worked hard to see this old dog soften his heart.

I began to have an increasing awareness of the softer aspects of God's nature, what some might allocate to being more "feminine," or at least I did. I thought about how the Bible says that "in His image he created them, *male and female* He created them."[13] I began to recognize, for the first time, components of the nature of God that I had not previously ascribed to him. The tender heart of God was pursuing me.

—

I mentioned earlier that I had been introduced to A.W. Tozer, a prolific author and preacher who pastored a church in Chicago in the 1940s and 1950s. He died in

---

13. Genesis 1:27

1963, the same year as C.S. Lewis. I read all of his books, and his teaching was the beginning of breaking down the walls of fundamentalism in my life, aka my "addiction to certainty."

Tozer had many memorable statements, but the one that stuck with me the most was "that everyone has as much of the Holy Spirit as they want." Wow, that means that if I am willing to pay the price, and make the sacrifices they have, I can live a life as amazing as those I looked up to.

When I moved to Denver, the church I attended in Littleton was a Swedish Baptist denomination. Unlike the Southern Baptists, they were much more open to mystery. The senior pastor even taught a class on spiritual gifts. This was one of my first steps away from fundamentalist thinking.

Rumor of an ex-Mormon believer spread through the Denver area and soon I had speaking engagements, starting with the Full Gospel Businessmen's Fellowship. These guys were very charismatic and I was prayed over "in tongues" for the first time. I didn't know what the heck was happening; it sounded like gibberish to me! But, at the same time, I wasn't repulsed.

They were all amazed that someone with my history could "find Jesus." Before too long, I was traveling to the outskirts of Denver, speaking with fellow businessmen about my life. I found myself stuck between feeling really good about myself and fighting my deep-seated insecurity. But for the first time, I started to see myself the way my Father in heaven did, and boy did it feel good. I was finally becoming that "new creation" I was reading about in the Bible. [14]

Before Rhonda's and my one-year anniversary, I got word that I was needed in California to run the Diagnostic Repair Center in Ontario. We had tickets for a trip to the British Isles with Rhonda's folks to celebrate our anniversary, so I decided to wait until after the trip to tell Rhonda. I didn't want to ruin our fun on that trip.

---

14. 2 Corinthians 5:17

CHAPTER NINE

A Fresh Start

Thankfully, Rhonda was all for the move. The wheels started turning and in July of 1988 we drove to southern California. My kid brother Stan wanted to visit a friend down near the beach, so he offered to use his Nissan pickup and help us move. The majority of our belongings went in the moving van, but Stan took the more fragile items in his truck and we followed in Rhonda's Subaru.

We were crossing the Rockies when the corner of Stan's tarp came loose. Rhonda and I had been enjoying a quiet time of reminiscing in her car, listening to "Mr. Colorado", Dan Fogelberg. I hopped out of the car to help Stan tie down the tarp, maximum two minutes. When I hopped back into Rhonda's car, I was animated and talking loudly at about a hundred miles an hour! Stan had that effect on me. He's very high energy and a barrel of fun. Rhonda was genuinely scared by the transformation.

GM put us in a hotel until we could find a place to live. During this time, Rhonda began having some health issues, and blacked out in a grocery store. The doctor determined it was her asthma acting up from the poor air quality. A friend told us about Lake Arrowhead, so we drove up one Sunday for lunch and were shocked by the cost of homes listed in the local real estate flyer. And, before long, we had found a cute little place with a tiny corner view of the lake. My new fifty-mile commute took me an hour each way, but I knew people whose five-mile commutes took just as long. At least I was moving the whole time.

We found a cute little Baptist church that had a vibrant music program. I had sung in the choir at our church in Denver and really enjoyed it. I even sang to Rhonda in our wedding. (I did have the song recorded in case I was too emotional to sing, but I managed to pull it off live.)

———

Like with the businessmen in Denver, I was soon asked to share my story and even lecture on Mormonism. I once lectured for six weeks in a row.

In retrospect, I'm shocked by some of the assumptions I made. I was still leaning toward legalism at the time, and had a long way to go. Someone asked me if I thought there were any believers in the Mormon church?

I emphatically said no, because if they got converted, the Holy Spirit would lead them out.

Looking back, I am more convinced now that a believer may be asked to stay married to a non-believing spouse rather than divorce. I find it closer to the heart of God that they would stay, preserve the family, and try to win the others over with their example of a changed and loving life.

I, for one, didn't know how to truly love until I accepted the love of God deep in my soul.

———

After about three and a half years in southern California, GM decided to take the anti-lemon law efforts of the Diagnostic Repair Center program and roll it out nationwide. They formed the Field Engineering program and we were supposed to be headquartered at a local GM Technical training center.

We had four salaried employees in Ontario and all but me were local and wanted to stay. I was glad to get out and head to the Northwest. The only problem was that the training center was in Portland and neither Rhonda nor I cared for what we'd seen of Portland. A friend of mine provided lemon law buy-back information that showed about twenty times more buy backs in Washington than Oregon. I convinced GM to let me locate in the Seattle area to service that larger population, and Rhonda picked out the charming waterfront town of Gig Harbor. She said it sounded cute.

We flew up and went house hunting with a real estate broker, looking for a house with at least a tiny view of the ocean. All the houses in our price range had shag carpet and dark paneling, basically needing approximately ten to fifteen thousand dollars in remodeling costs before they were livable. I had requested a two-car garage; we had no garage in Lake Arrowhead and I missed that.

After exhausting her list, we were about to cross the bridge into Tacoma when she mentioned one more house, but it only had one garage. It was a new spec home that had been on the market for three months. We decided to go have a look and—lo and behold—it had a two-car garage! The listing agent had entered the information wrong in the MLS. There it was, just waiting for us, brand new with two garage doors and seven hundred square feet of deck that looked out toward a breathtaking view of nearby Fox Island and Hales Passage, the water between the island and us. *WOW,* what an amazing opportunity!

We offered what the builder was asking and flew home to pack up. It felt like a wonderful blessing from God. We had prayed for a view and that was just what we got—a new home with a view. It was just like Jesus to exceed our wants and desires.

We moved in the weekend of Thanksgiving 1991 and started looking for a church to attend. Most of the churches we visited were so small, they were the type that once they discovered you had leadership or musical gifts, you were put in charge of the department. We were still working on having a baby and didn't feel like spending that much time "serving" was for us.

Then, in 1992, on the first Sunday of the new year, we visited PCF (Peninsula Christian Fellowship) and instantly fell in love with the worship, which was the most contemporary I had ever heard. One of the elders was speaking that Sunday and was rock solid. We came back—again and again.

After a few weeks, we noticed that even though we sat in four very different locations in the service, no one really approached us or tried to get to know us. We really felt like this was where we needed to be, and it was a good size, and it didn't have the same troubling issues as some others we had visited, so we made an appointment with the senior pastor. When we told him about his church not being very friendly, he surprised me by asking if we would stay and help fix that issue. It was an invitation I couldn't pass up, so that became our church home for the next six years.

Not very long after that, we heard the pastor speak about how the church had started: it had been a splinter from a more conservative church that didn't want contemporary music in the service. But the funny thing was that there were two major groups that had joined together. One group taught that speaking in tongues was from the devil and the other group taught that if you didn't speak in tongues, you might not even be saved at all!

Over the years, we observed a melding together of the two factions and the two extremes both moved to a more central position. The pastor told us about how he had made a deal with the Lord that if God put words in his mouth that were new to him, he would speak them out. Not long after that he received his prayer language (aka "speaking in tongues").

That sounded very logical to me, so I made the same deal with God. Not long afterward, I was driving to a meeting and I heard a word in my mind (I later found out it was Arabic for "praise"). I spoke the work out loud and instantly experienced a surge of what felt like electricity up my spine. When I asked aloud, "Is that you, God?" it happened again. One word, that's how it started. I was a card-carrying charismatic now, no turning back. [15]

—

15. I've since learned a new phrase: "Bapticostal," which really fits. Baptists are known for their knowledge of the Bible, and of course Pentecostals are known for being "Spirit-filled."

Understanding and embracing the softer side of God's attributes has made it easier for me to accept hard circumstances when they arise. It was a journey for me to learn that God wasn't always waiting to whack or correct me, and that trials weren't some form of judgment. This came up when Rhonda and I realized we wouldn't be able to have children of our own.

When my mom met Rhonda, the first thing she said to her was that I was going to make the best father. *Wow*, pretty high expectations and pressure. As it turned out, we weren't able to have children, and the last surgery Rhonda had almost killed her with septic shock. We explored adoption but every door was slammed in our faces.

Then Rhonda found a great book written by a pastor's wife who was infertile herself, *Childless Is Not Less*. In the book, the author chronicled her struggles in very honest and gut-wrenching detail. One section that hit us both was her story about prepping their church for a Mother's Day celebration. While setting up, the woman started to weep uncontrollably and ask in her heart, *God, what is going on here?* She felt like she was grieving but no one had died. Then God tenderly spoke that no one had lived.

That story still hits me hard; I'm actually blinking back tears as I write. For the first time, Rhonda and I felt like we had permission to grieve the death of a dream, and, in our case, a miscarried child. We had focused so much on being parents that we had lost sight of being a married couple. And we realized that our Father God, our loving Parent, cared for us in our grief.

The book finished with a chapter about being a "child-blesser." Without children of our own, we realized we had the time, energy, and resources to bless other people's children. We told God that if He left a baby on our doorstep we would take it in! But we also recognized that He is the giver of life, and He always knows best and works things out for our good. Besides, with the size of my family, all it would take was one tragic accident and we could have five or more children under our care!

With that major subject in our rearview mirror, we actually started talking about our individual dreams and desires. It turned out that Rhonda had studied youth ministry in college, and with my love for children, it became obvious to us both that we should start working with the youth at our church. Rhonda had read the *Childless Is Not Less* book to me on a trip to the Tetons for a marriage enrichment conference led by our friend H. Norman Wright. When we returned home, we sought out the youth pastor at our church to tell him we wanted to volunteer.

His response caught us off guard when he explained that, while we were gone, he had announced his resignation. WHAT?? *Very funny, God.* We had a few months to learn before he left, and we held the junior high and high school groups together once he did. Forty-odd hormone-engorged youth, what a life lesson.

This really caused me to read and dig into not only the Scriptures, but other trusted authors as well, including A.W. Tozer, C.S. Lewis, and George MacDonald. I read their books voraciously, and tried to teach what I was learning to our youth group kids at a level they could grasp and apply.

One axiom I have found true is that if you really want to understand something, try to teach it to someone else. I remember one sincere young girl who was an avid reader and asked why she had to read the Bible more than once? What a great question; she knew who the bad guy was and that the good guy won.

That same girl gave me a very poignant lesson one Sunday when the schedule was very busy and the pastor announced that they would forego communion, which they always did the first Sunday of the month, and do it the next week. She turned to me and asked, with shock in her voice, "Is that biblical?" Her tradition had become the way God wanted it done!

We so often fall into that same pitfall. It reminds me of the Sermon on the Mount where Jesus corrects the people's theological errors after two thousand years of what we call the Old Testament. How silly of us to think that we have Him all figured out two thousand years later. It is far more likely that a conversation with Jesus would be filled with His same words: "You've heard it said, but let Me tell you the truth."

———

One Sunday morning, Rhonda suggested that we do some role playing with the high school youth. I played the Mormon and they tried to convert me. That was a huge success; they would see us at a Wednesday night service and declare that they "had me," but then I would shoot them down the following Sunday.

This went on for weeks; sometimes I would invoke the Mormon biblical-escape hatch, that Joseph Smith didn't have time to correct all the errors in the Bible before he was killed. Mormons have their own version of the Bible called the Inspired Version, which includes the corrections that Joseph Smith made while using the "seer stones." For example, in John 1:1, it says, "The word was a god," not that the word *was* God. Smith also changed the Lord's Prayer from "Lead us not into temptation," to "Leave us not in temptation." He taught that in order to become a god, you had to be tempted in all things, yet without sin, like Jesus. Some changes are subtle, others not so much.

Of course, the kids thought that was a total cop out, but it's a reality you might face in witnessing to a Mormon, so I used it. After about six or seven weeks of their frustration rising, some of them asked how on earth I got saved. That was the kind of question we were after! I explained to them that salvation is the work of the Holy Spirit and it's different for everyone. Only God can change a person's heart.

I was also driving home the point of our unique path to God. There are no formulas that work effectively on either the masses or on individuals, in my opinion. When I want to share with someone how to find God, I suggest looking for the way God is already active in their life and gently fan the sparks into a flame. But this takes time to get to know them and build a relationship, which is foundational. To quote one of my former pastors: "Authority comes through relationship. You don't have a voice in my life unless I know how much you care."

Those years working with the youth were amazing. I highly recommend it to anyone who wants to impact the next generation. We have been blessed to be honorary grandparents to a handful of children of those youth we worked with. Rhonda still gets a handful of phone calls on Mother's Day, being honored by them. And the best part is, we don't have to pay for college.

—

We learned and grew tremendously at this church, Peninsula Christian Fellowship,. It was my first church home that was not "fundamentalist." Increasingly, in retrospect, I could see how the FLDS and the Christian fundamentalists I had encountered were not all that different: they were the only ones with the truth, so that meant they were the only ones going to heaven. They had an answer for everything; they had *certainty*. In either community, there was absolutely no room for doubt or uncertainty. You were called to "have a reason for hope that was in you."

Both groups have their favorite translation of the Bible: Inspired Version for the FLDS and the good old King James for the fundamentalist Christians. I was once given a book about the King James being the only acceptable version by a half sister who had been recently converted. I asked her if their missionaries taught tribal people Shakespearian English so they could understand the Bible. You could hear crickets.

CHAPTER TEN

Getting to Know My (Heavenly) Father

My spiritual journey had made me friends with Jesus, but God the Father was still pretty scary. After all, He was the one who would throw you into hell for all eternity if you didn't believe the correct stuff, right?

In this leg of my spiritual journey, I started to become aware of the Holy Spirit and how He works. I would say something when I was speaking that I hadn't really thought of before and would brush it off until someone came to me after and related how those specific words had impacted them. The Holy Spirit was speaking through me, *Wow!*

But the Trinity was still a complete mystery to me. I'd heard all the analogies, like "water in different states," or an egg, blah, blah, blah. But none of them would get past my logic gatekeeper. I remember finally resigning myself that it was a mystery I would understand in the next life and that was okay. I didn't need to have an answer; I could be comfortable with the "unknowing."

Wow, what a freedom. It was the beginning of trust, really the beginning of a mature faith. Fundamentalists, as I've said, are addicted to certainty. They have to know the answers, which explains some of the really weird stuff they come up with.

Joseph Smith made up a whole theology about three levels of heaven because the apostle Paul referenced being caught up to the "third heaven" in 2 Corinthians 12. In Hebrew terms, the third heaven simply meant the very presence of God. The first heaven is our sky and atmosphere and the second heaven is space. But there you go . . . it's a mystery. How do you explain (or attain with any predictability) the *very presence* of God? Fundamentalism just can't handle it.

Fundamentalists also like formulas, when the reality is that each of us comes to Jesus in a very unique way. There are no formulas. If you read the Gospels in the Bible (the books of Matthew, Mark, Luke, and John in the New Testament), you'll see Jesus never performed a miracle the same way twice: for one blind man, He spit in his eyes. Another one He made mud and rubbed it into the man's eyes, another was told to go wash in a specific stream. Jesus said He didn't do anything except what the Father told Him, in that moment.[16]

Recognizing all that, I now know that formulas and pat answers are definite signs of legalism and fundamentalism. Thomas the Doubter (Jesus' own disciple, who wasn't sure it was really Jesus he was seeing when Jesus appeared following His resurrection) was ridiculed in those circles, but I believe I would have been the same way. Jesus didn't rebuke Thomas for his uncertainty; He offered him proof. I think Thomas' doubts were just fine with Jesus, and you can see the fruit of that in Thomas' response; he dropped to his knees and declared, "My Lord and my God!"[17]

———

Our involvement with the youth at our local church soon led to me becoming a deacon. It was fun taking care of the practical stuff. It also meant we got to attend some pretty cool meetings.

Early one summer, a man from Tyler, Texas came to our church; his name was Don Crum. Don had an amazing ministry! He had been raised in the Church, and had believed most of his life. As Don tells the story, he was

---

16. John 8:28
17. John 20:28

sixteen years old and having a crisis of faith and decided to kill himself. He had a fairly large handgun aimed at his chest and pulled the trigger. But the bullet didn't hit him; it missed to the side and shot a hole in the brand-new shirt his mom had bought him. He joked that if he didn't kill himself his mom was going to do it for him

He attempted again, planting the barrel right against his chest and pulling the trigger, but the gun didn't fire. He opened the chamber of the gun and the primer had been pierced by the firing pin and had not gone off. This boy had been around guns all his life and had never, ever seen anything like that. He looked up to the sky and said, "God, if You're real, then show me." God obviously showed up in a big way, because that started an amazing ministry.

While still in high school, Don became the chaplain of the local hospital. The doctors actually came to him and asked him to quit praying for people because they were losing money! The operating rooms were scheduled and then going empty because people were walking out of the hospital completely healed. By the time Don came to see us, he was a grown man, had planted thirty-three churches in West Africa, and had established a school and a seminary there.

In his school and seminary in Africa, their normal practice was to go into the surrounding villages and do what they would call a "crusade." (I realize it is not politically correct these days to use that term.) They would stay for a period of time and train a local leader from the village, and then leave the people in his hands instead of coming in and putting in a white person in the middle of Africa to tell the people how they were supposed to become more like God. It was a very unique way of looking at it (in those days, anyway), and I personally thought it was brilliant.

So, after having dinner and hearing Don's story on a Thursday night, we had a special Friday night meeting at the church. Because I was one of the deacons, I was in charge of catching people. This was a charismatic church and had the practice of "slaying in the Spirit," where people are sometimes overcome by the power of the Holy Spirit and drop to the floor in a spiritual encounter with God. "Catchers" in a church service would make sure people didn't get hurt on the way down! Don wasn't like some evangelists that push people over; He would just tell you to raise your hands and he'd start to pray for you and—boom!—people would fall down. It was the most bizarre thing I'd ever seen.

While catching people, it was kind of odd because every once in a while somebody would just be really heavy. Not just like a big round guy "heavy," but they would be a lot more dense for their size. I nearly dropped the first person that was "heavy" like that. I had heard that the glory of God was often referred to as the "weightiness of God," and this made me think.

———

Friday night was followed up by a Saturday night meeting, and after I was done catching people that night I stood in line for prayer for myself. Honestly, I kind of had a feel for how long Don prayed for someone before they fell down. I paused and then leaned backward, was caught, and laid on the floor.

Sunday morning came and Don stood up and chastised the men for sitting in their seats while the women went forward to be prayed for. He accused the men of being afraid of letting go of control of their bodies, and not trusting God. That hit me between the eyes. I distinctly heard God say, "You know, if you fall down on your own, Howard, you're still in control."

That was a challenge I accepted. I said, *Okay, God, You'll have to knock me down then.* I went up and caught people after the service. Then it was time to pray for the deacons and other leaders who had been catching people. I planted my feet and I thought again, *Okay God, you're going to have to knock me over.* I didn't even feel myself tilt and woke up two hours later on the floor, weak as a kitten, barely able to crawl back to the pew.

The cool thing is that I wasn't just having a nice afternoon nap. I heard God say, "I love you, my son!" When I woke up, my ears were full of tears (I was laying on my back)—tears of joy to hear such an affirming statement from my heavenly Father.

Later that night, we had another service. This time Don decided he would start with the leaders instead of finishing up at the end. It's not that God runs out of anointing and the rest get leftovers. He just wanted some special focus time to pray and prophesy over each of us. He took some time to just kind of encourage us and speak words of life over us.

He spoke things about fathering over me, and then he prayed for me and I went down. In my mind's eye, I could see myself in a circle of friends and I was around seven years old. We were playing marbles. I glanced over my shoulder and saw God. He was about fifteen feet away and I shouted to the guys, "Look, that's my daddy, that's my daddy!" He put his arms out to me and I rushed into them, and he picked me up and gave me a big hug. While he was hugging me, he did something very personal—he tickled me. (I had done that for probably twenty years to my younger brothers and sisters and nephews and nieces. I'd scooped them up in my arms and then tickle them when they couldn't get away.)

That imagery was a very personal statement. Later I realized it meant he'd had his eye on me for a long, long time and he knew me very intimately. I was sitting in his lap, still a child, and he was stroking his fingers affectionately through my hair, rubbing my cheek and just loving on me. Then he said it was time to go, but of course I didn't want to go. "Can I just stay here?" I asked.

He told me, "I want you to share this with other people." I told him okay, and asked if I could come back. He said yes, and I hopped down off his lap.

I woke up and I was still kind of giggling a little bit from being tickled by God. The guy next to me was waking up and also laughing. We crawled our way over to a pew and propped ourselves up. I asked him why he was laughing because I knew why I was laughing. We sat there laughing and laughing about how funny and how good God was to us, his little boys.

—

I had been on the floor for two hours and decided I should get up and catch some people. Don told us about an experience in Mexico where people would walk by the building where he was ministering and they would fall down just on their own. Many would fall like a tree and smack their heads on the concrete so violently the paramedics would rush to check them out. They would wake up without even a goose egg. He warned us that if we were falling down on our own, we shouldn't get mad if we get hurt. "If God knocks you down," Don told us, "you will be fine."

I walked behind a person waiting for prayer, ready to catch. Don saw me and told me to put my hands up. Again I didn't even remember tilting. I was in a dark room with hints of light around the edges. God was hovering over me with His hands on my chest like He was going to give me CPR. When He pushed down on my chest, it felt like bolts of electricity were surging through my body. All my muscles tensed and it didn't hurt, but it was a pretty intense sensation.

I asked Him what he was doing, and He said, "Shuuuuush, I'm doing a deep work in you." I woke up from that probably forty-five minutes later, exhausted and spent, but full of joy and hope and peace and love— all those good things to the brim.

It was a while before I noticed that I wasn't praying to Jesus any more. For the first time, I was praying to my Father in heaven, even calling him Papa at times. He was no longer the mean old man upstairs that was going to send me to hell if I messed up. He was now my loving Father who has known me and watched me and worked in my life to bring me into a close loving relationship with him. This relationship allows me to trust him with all my heart and be comfortable with "mystery," especially the mystery of the next life spent with him, where there is no more pain and no more tears—except maybe the good kind that are filling my eyes as I write this.

—

Back then, after my first encounters with my heavenly Father, being the spiritually proud man that I was, I assumed that, when God said he wanted me to share that experience with people, He wanted me to pray for people and they would fall down, just like Don had done. Well, that wasn't what he had in mind. He wanted me to share how much he loves each one of us, and how intimately familiar he is with our ways, and that he adores each and every one of us.

The cool thing about the deep work he did in me was he shattered a hard heart and gave me a tender heart in its place. My wife often comments that I cry more at movies now than she does, always wiping away tears from my eyes as something hits my heart and my spirit, and just moves me at the strangest times. It reminds me of the title of C.S. Lewis' autobiography, *Surprised by Joy*. God's joy keeps sneaking up on me and it makes me catch my breath. This is probably what set me up for the next work God wanted to do in me.

Our friends Marty and Debbie and their family moved to Gig Harbor, Washington from Lakeside, Montana. They were hired as the youth pastor at PCF, rescuing me and Rhonda. As a YWAM leader (Youth with a Mission), Marty had one remaining obligation that summer: the "Youth Attack" mission trip.

The Lakeside YWAM base is on Flathead Lake by Kalispell, Montana—beautiful. That year, Rhonda and I attended as part of the group of fifty-three high school students and thirteen adult leaders. During the team-building time, Dave Gustafson, who is a brother-in-law to Marty, came and spoke to the team about the father heart of God. It was two and a half days of amazing training.

The afternoon before we were leaving for Tijuana, Mexico for our mission trip, there was a time set up for ministry. We talked to several of those kids and they had horrific stories: Mom committed suicide and Dad checked out, and other things that were very difficult to hear and share and embrace with those young people. So, when the time for ministry came (i.e., taking requests for people wanting prayer), and nobody spoke up, I was thinking, *Hey you, and you and you!* I knew a dozen people who needed to stand up and get healing for their relationship with their father. But it didn't happen that way.

The daughter of the worship leader at our church stood up and talked about how her dad was always at the church and she felt like she was less important than church was and what a wound that had been to her heart. Now, I have to admit I hadn't had the best first impression of her. She was one of the "cool" kids and she always kind of wanted preferential treatment, so when Rhonda and I started working with the youth she had expected that same treatment. We wouldn't give it to her so she just kind of wrote us off—so I wrote *her* off. But hearing about her wound from her father just broke my heart—I could relate!—and I heard God tell me to ask her to forgive me. All I could think was, *Wait, I'm one of the leaders.* He insisted I do it anyway.

So, I went up to her after we prayed for her, and I asked her to forgive me. She gave me the biggest, sweetest hug. On the way back to my seat, nobody else was saying anything, and I heard God tell *me* to forgive *my* dad.

But I *had* forgiven my dad—well, sort of. I distinctly remember forgiving him for raising me as a "plyg kid." But I realized in that moment there was more forgiving to be done.

With no one else responding, I told Dave that God was telling me to forgive my dad, but that I thought I had. So Dave advised me to just start processing out loud. I started to tell God how I remembered forgiving my father for raising me as a plyg kid. Then it hit me like a truck! I had a vision of being a five-year-old little boy climbing up on my dad's lap and having him push me off, because he was watching TV. I'd always given him a pass for not being there with twenty-seven kids (How could anyone?) But there was a little boy inside me who needed healing.

I forgave my dad for not being there, for loving football and TV and anything else more than me. The tears that came washed me clean! I was instantly surrounded by the youth, praying for me and pouring out their love. This was the most cleansing time of renewal in my life. And, it had long-term fruit in my relationship with my dad.

I did have a relationship with him. In fact, I was the only one of my father's twelve boys who called him on his birthday and on Father's Day (well, my brother Phil probably wished him a happy birthday too, but he lived downstairs from Dad so that didn't count as much). I would tell him I loved him and he would say, "I know."

But after I forgave him, I called Dad on the phone and told him I loved him, and this time he said, "I love you too, son." Before this, my need and requirement in my "I love you" was likely sending up red flags to him. After that, we had an amazing relationship that got even better over the years.

I can only imagine what he went through trying to provide for twenty-seven mouths that needed feeding, plus keeping three women happy. I think the man deserved a medal.

—

Immediately after forgiving my dad, I felt this amazing lightness. I was no longer striving to get my dad's attention and approval. I didn't have to win anymore. I used to try to win at all costs, all that mattered was that I was winning! If I was a winner, maybe my dad would notice and say something nice; never-mind that he was a thousand miles away.

I remember that my striving got particularly ugly during a Thanksgiving turkey bowl game with the youth group, where the youth workers were playing against the adults in the church. One of the women decided we should let the girls play, of all things! I distinctly remember yelling at an eighty-pound girl for missing a block, and thinking to myself, *Oh my God, Howard; it's only a game,* but still being unable to stop. *Where did that come from?*

My reality was that growing up with eleven brothers in a dominantly sports-oriented family meant there was constant competition. The older brothers would pit their younger brothers against each other, whether it was boxing, football, wrestling, or horseback riding. You name it, we competed.

There was also a pecking order that was established, based on success and failure. We lived out the old adage that second place was the first loser. Ridicule, bullying, and name calling was the prize for being defeated. It was my brothers, not schoolmates, who called me "Howeird." It's no wonder that we all have fought our own battles with insecurity.

In our family, with us triplets, Shem was the champion of all things athletic, and I was the smart one who was a confident public speaker, which left David with the leftovers. We were brutal as only kids can be. I want to publically apologize to Dave and ask his forgiveness for how I saw and treated him. He's turned out amazingly well given the start we gave him. He's a gifted craftsman and has a huge heart and brilliant mind. Love you, Dave.

There was spiritual competition as well. We were praised for being able to "share our testimony" during family home evening (a weeknight event used to indoctrinate the youngest into how to act and speak). If we could sing well, we won! If we didn't get nervous speaking in front of a group, we won! Recite a religious poem, you won!

Perfection was required, even demanded: "Be ye perfect as your Father in heaven is perfect," was an out-of-context scripture we were reminded of regularly. Unfortunately, as children, we had no idea that our parents weren't perfect, far from it. We piled mountains of condemnation onto ourselves, for deep inside we knew we were never going to be good enough.

To this day, I'm convinced that if, years ago, I hadn't asked that sweet young gal at that youth retreat to forgive me, I might've missed that chance to forgive my dad and experience freedom from this issue. That knowledge sure taught me an important lesson: obedience first. The opportunity may or may not have come up again—and if it did, I might not be ready or in the right frame of mind or spirit to hear what my heavenly Father wanted to say to me—and that wasn't a conversation I'd ever want to miss.

That fall after I forgave my father, I was at a men's retreat playing football. I wanted to just play on the line, but my teammates insisted I play quarterback. The game went back and forth and the other team scored the final touchdown, putting them ahead when the dinner bell rang. I started walking off the field, not caring that we would lose the game if we quit now. My teammates insisted that we get one more chance to tie the game. So I threw a long touchdown pass and we all walked to dinner. They were happy and I didn't care; it was a very unusual feeling. That wasn't like the old me at all!

Later that year, I was playing volleyball with the youth group, and one of the girls came up and told me how much she enjoyed playing volleyball with me. The way she said it made me inquire—why? She explained that she used to pretend she was sick so she wouldn't have to play with me, because I would yell at her when she missed the ball!

Looking back on this topic has made me understand a lot about myself. I've realized that I was trained to be a perfectionist. The irony of it all is that I didn't require perfection of myself, just others around me. I had a highly trained critical eye; I could see imperfections at a glance. As an automotive technician, that was very practical and helpful. I was rewarded and praised for that skill.

As a human being, brother, and husband, I didn't realize that by pointing out everyone else's imperfections, those around me thought I was also judging them as well.

I must confess this has been a very recent insight that has surfaced in the process of writing this story of my life. I'm generally a positive person. I've dealt with my past hurts, forgiven those involved, and moved on. Admittedly, going back and revisiting the pains and hurts of my childhood has been difficult. (If my memory doesn't match with those of my siblings, I apologize. I'm trying to make this telling of my life as real and transparent as I can.)

I feel completely loved and accepted by my heavenly Father, and have a new heart to be able to express that love and acceptance to other people. I have apologized to Rhonda for my critical spirit and how I must have hurt her over the years.

When I did this, she teared up and told me she had resolved herself that I was who I was and that's how it always would be. She had given up and resigned herself to living with a man like that. Rhonda asked forgiveness for giving up on believing I had the capacity to change. And I've asked God to help me and have seen change—even (and especially) while I'm driving!

CHAPTER ELEVEN

Grace:
My New Normal

While all this was happening in my personal and spiritual life, there was a lot going on in my workplace life as well. God was changing everything up!

I'd had a great job with General Motors for sixteen years—I had a fat salary, a company car, and all the credit card debt to go along with the lifestyle. For nearly ten of those years, GM was twisting my arm to go to Michigan. All promotions were in Michigan. I'd visited Michigan at almost every time of year, and I didn't find any of it appealing in any of them. The humidity was so severe you needed fish gills to breathe! And the winters were bitterly cold and then some. So, all that to say, Michigan wasn't an option for me. I told Rhonda after six months in Gig Harbor, back in 1991, that I would leave GM before leaving Gig Harbor. I didn't know how prophetic that would become.

In 1998, when GM restructured their field operations and eliminated three thousand jobs in the forty-eight states, they were looking for volunteers to leave the company and take the golden handshake, which for me was six figures because of the sixteen years of service. Basically, they offered to pay me "not to go to Michigan." That's when I raised my hand and said, "Pick me, pick me!"

As of January 1, 1999, I was unemployed for the first time in my life. Part of the separation package was fifteen months of continued salary, so I had some time to figure things out. I had talked to a couple dozen dealers about providing a link on their website that would go directly to me, so if a person called the dealership asking for tech help for their GM vehicle, they could just refer them to the website and my link. I thought I would get a few hundred dealers signed up for a minimal retaining fee and be set.

But after I left GM and contacted the dealers, it turned out that most didn't have their own websites. They only had the basic website that GM provided them, with a map, address, business hours, etc.—and GM didn't allow them to put any links on those sites. So I was back to square one!

Randomly, I ran into an old friend in Costco of all places. Ed worked for Power Distributing, a diesel supply business that also trained the new systems to their independent repair shops. I had worked with Ed when GM came out with the electronically controlled diesel injection pumps for the 1994 model year trucks. He knew all the pump information and I knew the vehicle side.

As we caught up on life and work, Ed told me they were very excited to get trained on the Ford Powerstroke diesel pickup trucks. Their association of independent diesel shops had been approached by an engineer with Caterpillar who had designed the hydraulic/electronic controlled injectors. I asked Ed how many techs he'd trained and he proudly declared twenty. When I asked how many were working on those trucks, he hung his head and said none. I told him I knew why, which perked him up. "They are afraid of electricity, that's why." Ed was stunned and asked how I knew that. By working with diesel techs at dealerships for twenty-five years!

When I left Costco that day, I had an offer to train Ed's technicians in electricity, electronics, and scan tool diagnosis of those trucks. I went straight to Radio Shack and bought power supplies, switches, bulbs, resistors, transistors, etc., and produced training boards for the first class.

Ed was so excited about getting training for his customers that he invited the training coordinator for ADS (Association of Diesel Specialists) to attend the first class. Mike managed a similar business in Denver and was so enthused by the training that he got me a national contract with ADS. So, for about eighteen months, I flew around the country training diesel mechanics in electricity and electronic control systems.

But in the fall of 2000, when the economy slowed way down, they quit signing up for classes and I found myself unemployed again. Sure, I fixed a few cars in my garage at home but not enough to pay the bills. So, I applied for work at the dealerships I knew. Unfortunately, with my four-year degree and all my GM technical experience, most of those guys were afraid I would have their jobs in six months and they would be the ones looking for work! I was unemployed for almost a year.

That was one of the most difficult periods in my life. As someone who prided himself on being a good provider, a lot of things that I put my self-worth in were stripped away. It would be an understatement to say this was a very humbling time. My A+ credit was stripped down to an F! I couldn't get any help. It was pretty desperate.

One shining light was that I was working on the personal cars of the police lieutenant in Gig Harbor, who kept asking me when I was going to open a shop so he could bring me the patrol cars. I decided to take him up on the challenge.

I found a few "hole in the wall" low-rent spots, but none of them were within city limits, so that wouldn't work for the police fleet. I finally found a little shop with enough room for three cars or two trucks in Gig Harbor.

Honestly, I felt like I was going back twenty-five years to when I was a mechanic right out of high school.

Little did I know I was squarely in the middle of God's grace.

———

I didn't realize the difference it would make to have my own business. For the first time, I was able to set the workplace culture and treat customers the way I thought they should be treated. The business took off like wildfire.

I had to hire some help and soon was able to snatch our house out of foreclosure, and we're still in that home to this day. With my credit destroyed, I couldn't get any business loans, and it was literally hand to mouth for a long while. I felt like I was fifty feet underwater. But for me bankruptcy wasn't an option. I had taken people's money and spent it, and I didn't think it was right for me to just back out because I had a hard patch. So, as time went on and the business thrived, I paid everybody back! I made good on all of my debts and dug myself out of the hole with a lot of help and a lot of grace.

Another amazing story of grace came as I was making a final payment on the catch-up part of my mortgage. I woke up two days before a fifteen hundred-dollar payment had to be sent (by Western Union) and was racking my brain of who I knew who could lend me fifteen hundred dollars for a week. We had work in the shop, but it wasn't going to be done in time to make that last payment. I was so close and really stressing.

Then I heard God say to me, "You tell people you trust me, but do you really?" *Wow, gut check.*

I said, "Okay God, I'm letting go of this and trusting you," and I put it out of my mind. Early that morning, I got a call from the police lieutenant who had arranged for me to service their fleet. He had another Crown Vic broken down and wondered if I could squeeze him in that day. We did, and the bill came to $1,634. When he came to get the car, he took the invoice and was half-way out the door when he stopped, turned around, and asked if I wanted him to put it on his city credit card?

"I didn't know you had one of those," I replied.

"I do," he told me. "It's for emergencies."

Then it hit me: I would have the money I needed in the bank in two days, just in time, and the amount covered the fifteen hundred dollars plus the credit card fee and my ten percent tithe. *WOW.* (The reason I hadn't seen this as God's answer at first was because the city only paid bills every two weeks on Tuesdays, and to get paid on that Tuesday, you had to have it processed by the Friday before.)

That occasion was the only time the police chief used the card to pay for automotive repairs—and God used it to prove to me that I could trust him for any of my financial needs in the future!

———

Those are only a few stories of the ways that "grace" became my new normal.

There are so many other ways that freedom from the need for certainty, and the need to judge, has changed my life.

After I met and got to know Jesus in a deep and personal way, I was intoxicated by this idea of grace. It seemed almost miraculous to me (grace IS a miracle, really!) that I did not have to *earn* my salvation—that my salvation was in fact, a *free* gift from God. When I was a member of the FLDS church, my life's greatest focus was on measuring up, being good enough, and making all the correct choices. However, even then, I knew deep down inside that no matter what I did, it would never be enough.

At first, learning that Jesus doesn't have favorites—that he loves us all equally—seemed to right that wrong, so to speak. But the more time I spent in fundamentalist circles after I came to know Jesus, the more I began to pick up another form of elitist mentality that looked down on others (even others who believed in Jesus).

In the first group, we were taught to judge those *crazy* Charismatics. *Speaking in tongues? Certainly that was from the devil!* I was even given a book from someone at my church providing "proof" that speaking in tongues was the devil's work.

Next to judge were those Nazarenes, because they didn't believe that once you were saved, you were always saved. *You can lose your salvation? Blasphemy!*

> "You know you have remade Jesus in your own image when He hates all the same people you hate."
> —Anne Lamott

I also believed I was better than any group that was not "post-tribulation millennialist." With this perspective, how you understood the Book of Revelation, the hardest and least understood book in the Bible, now became of the utmost importance in determining if you were really saved, or just thought you were.

As time went on, this list of restrictions grew—until soon, I was right back in a legalistic stranglehold that put nearly everyone around me in a tight little box of my own making, even God. Was this really what I had signed up for when I surrendered my life to Jesus? Didn't I turn to Him to save me from striving and fear?

Over time, my focus had subtly shifted from worshiping Jesus to making sure my doctrine was correct and the very "best." I was obsessing over whether or not the things I believed were "right" or not (otherwise, I was believing a false gospel and would burn in hell for all of eternity). I had to have the correct version of Jesus, all the way down to the correct version of the Bible (because, of course, I believed there was only one).

Once, I was even told that I was going to burn in hell because I had versions of the Bible that weren't King James! I'd been threatened with burning in hell when I left the FLDS and actually resigned myself to the fact that it could quite possibly be my fate. Now, here I was again, yet this time as a born-again Christian, and the same thing was being held over my head! *What the hell?* (No pun intended!)

Although I knew that I was "saved by grace," I slowly and surely fell into the same patterns I'd been operating in before. Be sure to read my Bible every day, make sure to get to church the moment it opened (as often as possible), confessing my sins *openly* (called "accountability"), and so many other dos and don'ts that I couldn't possibly name them all.

Even as a follower of Jesus, I was consumed with striving and fear. The joy of the gospel was drained out of me, yet all of us at the church would rejoice when someone got "saved." We'd marvel at their enthusiasm and bold testimony, and then a sage would declare that it wouldn't last. How true and sad it was. Of course it wouldn't last—keeping up with the rules was a full-time job!

What freedom to learn that God doesn't keep score!

Another way I believe grace has changed me is in how I relate to my friends who don't share the same faith as me, or maybe who don't even ascribe to any faith at all. I often discuss with people who like to discuss these types of things what "salvation" really means to me now. I think it's less to do with our eternal inheritance and more to do with being saved from the person we would've been without Jesus. Without the Holy Spirit's compass in our lives, I dread to think of the selfish, angry, violent man I might have been. But the Lord saved me from myself.

I've mentioned how much I admire British author/theologian C.S. Lewis; I think I've read everything he published. In *Mere Christianity,* he made a statement that, "Nobody's one hundred percent Christian and nobody's zero percent Christian." I'm inclined to agree.

I'd rather refer to myself as a "follower of Jesus" than a Christian. I'm pretty sure most people understand why. Looking back, I see the hand of God working in my life long before I surrendered to him, and I also see him working in my friends' and family's lives, whether they recognize it or not.

CHAPTER TWELVE

Embracing the Mystery

One thing I've come to appreciate since I've gained freedom from my "addiction to certainty" is the beauty and wonder of mystery. There's a proverb in the Bible that says that God enjoys hiding things and it's the job of kings to search them out.[18] Similarly, it's been proven that a truth discovered stays with you for the length of your memory, but a truth told to you can sometimes take eight tellings before it's remembered long term.

Sometimes we need to live with the tension of not knowing, or not knowing fully, while we are in the process of discovering. Releasing our need for certainty, and embracing mystery, requires a significant level of

_____
18. Proverbs 25:2

humility. You have to become comfortable with "I don't know," or, "I may be wrong." For many of us, that's a difficult thing to say quietly to ourselves, much less out loud.

To deal with that tension, it is human nature to look for absolutes. We draw lines in the sand, and then we use those boundaries (many or most of which we have made up ourselves) to judge and condemn others who don't live with the same self-imposed restrictions or ideals. That's what judging others does: it reinforces the lines around you that you think are keeping you safe.

At the time, I didn't think my fundamentalist beliefs made me rigid. I thought they made me right! When you think having a very particular belief system is your salvation, you aren't likely to find it constricting. You're likely to find it comforting and empowering. And, when you think a particular belief system is also the only salvation for everyone else on the earth, you aren't likely to feel smug while imposing that view on others. You're likely to feel like their savior. That's one of the most dangerous undersides of the addiction to certainty.

——

The older I get, the more I realize how little I really know—and it's humbling. I've heard some people joke that they are proud of how humble they've become, which is an oxymoron. Humility is like a slippery fish: it's hard to hang on to once you even get a glimpse of it! Too many have confused humility with self-hatred, or a low self-esteem. Those are actually opposites.

Humility is not necessarily thinking better of others than you do yourself. It's more akin to meekness—which isn't mildness, but actually power under extreme control. You are powerful, impressive, and worthy of honor if for no other reason than you were created in the image of God. So, humility is simply being willing to be known by Him and others in the most truthful way you can, to take off the mask, the false front, the embellishments that make you seem better than you are.

> "We teach what we know, but reproduce who we are."
> —A.W. Tozer

I used to tell people I played college football, when in fact I tried out for the team and went through three-a-day practices for two weeks, only to find out that I didn't make the travel squad, much less qualify for a scholarship. That all changed when I became painfully aware of how much I struggled with pride. I was cocky and arrogant as a defense mechanism against the deep insecurity I felt growing up as a plyg kid. But the pride was a whole different beast. It actually fed my need for certainty. I was proud of how much I knew and enjoyed having an answer for everything. I was the "go-to guy" for answers.

One day, when reading the Bible, my regular reading brought me to 1 Corinthians 13, the "Love Chapter." I've read it so many times I could have quoted most of it. For some reason, that day I stopped and asked God to show me something new. Then, as I read the first verse about being able to speak many languages . . . but not having love; I felt God stop me and ask, "Love for whom?" I didn't know, so I kept reading, and he asked me again, "Love for whom?" Again after verse three, the same question.

I finally admitted I didn't know whom . . . and then I heard, "Those who don't!" So I re-read those verses and asked myself what would keep me from loving people, especially those who believed differently than me, and the answer he gave we was *pride:* pride in my knowing, pride in my spiritual gifts, and pride in what I'd received, my belongings. He was knocking at the door of my heart, waiting for me to open up.

Another thing that kept me securely trapped in the pride cycle was my fear of humiliation. The Bible says that God resists the proud and gives grace to the humble.[19]

I used to think that meant if I asked God for help with my pride, he would teach me by humiliating me. That was a lie from the pit of despair.

My awareness of my pride started to haunt me. I could see its strain on my marriage and every other significant

---

19. Proverbs 3:34; 1 Peter 5:5-6

relationship I had. Out of desperation, I prayed for God's help and what I received was the furthest thing from humiliation, and a major step forward in my process of loving myself. I've since coined a phrase: Once you've seen God, you're no longer impressed with yourself. And once you know how much He loves you, you no longer have a need to impress others.

When you are humble, you can be free to embrace the uniqueness of who you are, discover your truest strengths, and along with those, your corresponding weaknesses. As I grew to know my Heavenly Father AS a father, and became convinced of his love, I no longer saw my weaknesses as reasons for God to punish me. I no longer ducked or flinched when considering those things. I no longer had a need to feel "certain" that I'd found

"When you think having a very particular belief system is your salvation, you aren't likely to find it constricting. You're likely to find it comforting and empowering. And, when you think a particular belief system is also the only salvation for everyone else on the earth, you aren't likely to feel smug while imposing that view on others. You're likely to feel like their savior. That's one of the most dangerous undersides of the addiction to certainty."

—Howard Mackert

"the right way" or the "ultimate truth," or that I needed to impose it on others.

Rather, I've found that I have a Father who loves me more than I'll ever comprehend this side of eternity. And the coolest thing is that he loves us all the same way. There is nothing you can do to make God love you more—no church attendance, tithing or other giving, (even though they can be beneficial), no rosary beads, or especially self-recrimination or self-hatred—will ever make God love you any more than he does right now.

If you have children, think of how much you love them and then multiply that by infinity! God the Father and Jesus knew what it would cost them to make a way back to them and went through with the plan anyway, *Wow!*

———

Once I became secure in His love, along came trust—the elusive word that is experientially absent in too many of our life experiences. Trust is knowing I don't have to know the future without knowing that it's all going to work out. Granted, that can be hard, but hard things bring out the best in us.

As I grow in trust, my addiction to certainty is dying out and I like it. Comfort with mystery has taken its place. I no longer look at people with other lifestyles and think they are simply going to burn forever, and therefore don't deserve my respect, understanding, or honor.

Some people I know have quoted scriptures to me supporting that one sin or another is an "abomination," but I've found a list of *seven* things listed in the Bible that God says are an abomination to Him: "There are six things the LORD hates—no, seven things he detests: haughty eyes, a lying tongue, hands that kill the innocent, a heart that plots evil, feet that race to do wrong, a false witness who pours out lies, a person who sows discord in a family."[20] Notice that those are all "sins of the soul," to quote C.S. Lewis, rather than sins of the flesh, the animal side of who we are.

The judgment of others is something God will work out, not me. I no longer look at people begging in the streets with disdain. I used to think and have even sometimes told them to "go get a job." I'm now more inclined to wonder about the path they've walked that brought them there and remember the old adage that "except for the grace of God, so go I." All that is good in my life is a gift so what do I have to be proud about? I'm now more inclined to pray and possibly give them some cash.

---

20. Proverbs 6:16-19

By nature, I suppose I've always been a bit of a zealot. When I was in FLDS, I owned a full set of *The Truth* magazine, published by the Mussers in Salt Lake City, which held the troublesome "prophecy" that any of the apostles could receive revelation for the church, not just the head of the priesthood. (That's what caused the split at Short Creek in the 1980s.) I bought my own copy of the *Journals of Discourses*, which was about thirty hardbound volumes of all the sermons given at conferences held by the early Mormon church fathers from the time of Joseph Smith's martyrdom. It had the teachings of Brigham Young and many other Mormon leaders.

Even when I was wrong, I've always poured myself into what I believed. I love learning—it makes me feel alive! As you might guess, when reading teachings from that many men about the new religion (LDS), statements would often contradict each other and I would catch those potential conflicts as I read. I'd take these to my dad and ask him for an explanation, but his response was always simply to "put it on a shelf," and expect that when God revealed more light and knowledge to me, then I'd understand.

As a new Christian, I was facing similar contradictions: did the rooster crow twice or three times after Peter denied Jesus? (Why wasn't this stuff more consistent and precise?) Why does only one Gospel say that Jesus went into the wilderness to be tempted? The Gospel of Mark says the day after Jesus' baptism, he went to Peter's house in Galilee and healed his sick wife. Did he, really? (If you look at a map of the Holy Land, you'll see that you can't get to Galilee that quickly on foot from the area near Jericho where Jesus was baptized.)

You see, I had been conditioned for *certainty*. And as I've emphasized in this book, the need for certainty is the calling card for fundamentalists, whether they are Mormon or Christian or anything else. There is no room for doubt, no room for uncertainty. As a fundamentalist, you have to have an answer for everything, even if that answer is made up. The better I became at making up answers, the "wiser" I was considered. And of course, I became wise in my own eyes, a dangerous condition to be sure.

———

These days, my outlook on life is a lot greyer (in a good way), less black and white, since I have released my need for certainty and embraced the uncertainty of mystery. I believe spiritual pride is the worst kind of elitism there is. It is what Jesus railed on the Pharisees about all the time. They prayed in the streets with loud voices so everyone would see how holy they were, while the whole time their hearts were like a whitewashed tombs, Jesus told them.[21]

---

21. Matthew 23:27-28

The other insidious thing about pride is that it blinds us to its very existence. The more proud we are, the less we know it. Ask anyone who is in a legalistic group and they'll say they are defending the truth. I believe every one of us should honestly ask God to reveal any spiritual pride in our lives. (Do it, and it will be one of the best gifts you'll ever receive.)

But you might say, "Wait a minute, I said the 'sinner's prayer.' I'm going to Heaven because I'm forgiven." Are you sure? What about the verse where Jesus says that if you don't forgive, you won't be forgiven?[22] Let that sink in. We all need "orthopraxy" (right actions) as well as "orthodoxy" (right thoughts). In the book of James, we read that "faith without works is dead."[23]

Too many "believers" have seen accepting Jesus as the finished job, rather than the beginning of the process of salvation. Part of what he saves us from is a godless version of ourselves! C.S. Lewis said that "God loves us so much that He is committed to make us loveable." That takes more work for some of us than others.

When I'm feeling sorry for myself because life feels tough, I try to remember that God is trying to make me more loveable. I'm trying to ask more regularly, "What is the discomfort I'm feeling intended to teach me? What

---

22. Matthew 6:14-15
23. James 2:20

blind spot is being exposed?" We are all on our own journey, and who is to say that you are further along than the person next to you? We don't know their starting point, or the path they have been asked to walk, or even the consequences of their bad decisions versus our bad ones.

———

I'm reminded, too, of how uniquely Jesus worked. As I mentioned earlier, he healed four different blind people and didn't do it the same any two times. The point is that he reaches out to each of us in a very unique way; after all, we are all unique. There are no duplicates, not even with identical twins.

So I'll say it again: please beware of formulas. When someone hands you a formula, like "three simple steps to God . . ." or, "This magic prayer and you're in . . ." be assured that God doesn't work that way. Don't fall for what looks like an easy fix. The reality is that the gift is free, but it will cost you everything.

Jesus said that anyone who tries to save his or her own life will lose it, but if we lay down our lives, we will gain fullness of life.[24] This is a mystery to our minds and not easy to perceive. That's why it takes us our whole lives to understand.

_____

24. Matthew 16:25

As I continue to process these things and learn to live them out, I find I don't believe things many things I preached twenty years ago, or even ten years ago. I'm growing in understanding and awareness, along with humility. I don't doubt that many who read this will have strong objections to that. That's completely fine with me; I'm not the One who knows and sees.

We might be closer to agreement in the future and I look forward to that day, whether I begin to understand like you or the other way around. These are just thoughts from my journey and all I ask is that you test the fruit of this belief: Today, I'm far more loving, slower to judge, more compassionate, more patient, and maybe even less proud. In short (I hope), slightly more like Jesus.

———

People ask me how I make peace with how I was raised, and how I can be in such close relationship with family members who inflicted what we now know to be injustices on me and my siblings. My answer is one word: *grace.* Judgment belongs to God, and He gave it all to Jesus, the One who came to make a way back to the Father. Jesus clearly stated that he didn't come into the world to judge the world, but to save it, which he is actively doing.[25]

---

25. John 3:16-17

Judgment is his responsibility, not mine—at least, not in this life.

I believe that Jesus is the Way, Truth, and the Life, and that no one comes to the Father except through him,[26] but too many of my church friends have Jesus standing in the way like a traffic cop or the Nazi Gestapo asking for papers, or if you know the password. I like to see him standing with arms wide open, welcoming anyone who would freely come to him, freely extending forgiveness to me—and to others.

I have become convinced that God knows how to get what He wants; it's my pride and lack of trust in His goodness that make me doubt that. God IS good and He's in a good mood all the time. If you haven't read the book *The Shack*, by Wm. Paul Young, please do yourself a favor and read it. Let it pierce your heart with the truth that "God is especially fond of you" right here, right now, no matter where you are or what you're doing. Then turn around and be a vessel of that fondness so others can experience it too, through you.

I used to think that God was repulsed by my sin, but I'm reminded of the story of Samson in the Bible who was "lying with a prostitute in a Philistine town," and when the Philistines came to capture him, the Holy Spirit fell on him and he tore the city gates off their hinges

---

26. John 14:6

and escaped. *What?* He was clearly sinning and yet that didn't repel the Holy Spirit.

We really don't know much about God at all. But, luckily, Jesus said, "If you've seen me, you've seen the Father."[27] Remember the Father, Son, and Holy Spirit don't play good cop, bad cop. They are united—one in purpose—and that purpose is to eventually make you and me just like them: "glorious to behold, without spot or wrinkle."[28] (I like that wrinkle one more and more the older I get.)

Guess what? We can treat people like they are glorious today, right now. Look for it in others. You might have to look closely, but it's there, just a hint in their smile or the corner of their eye, or the touch of their hand, but it is there.

To those of us who consider ourselves "church people," let's look for God's activity in people—all people—and fan the sparks we see into a flame, and maybe at the right time pour gasoline on the flame. But let's never douse it out. Our judgment and criticism, our need to feel and impose certainty, can so easily extinguish those little flames. But most importantly, be constantly looking. God is actively at work in each one of us whether we are aware of Him or not.

---

27. John 14:9
28. Ephesians 5:27, New Living Translation

"Fear is a powerful motivator, but just perpetuates
failure. Only love brings breakthrough
and lasting change. It's about what we are
focusing on. Remember how deeply you are
loved by the one who knows you best."
—Howard Mackert

A cool example of this is my ninety-seven-year-old mother. A few years back she was feeling down, which was not a common thing. When asked, she said she was worried about the afterlife and her pending judgment. I asked her if she knew how much God loved her, and she replied no.

I then started to just speak "words of life" to her about how crazy God is about her. That he is smiling down on her and appreciates her steadfastness. I used the phrase I read in *The Shack*, that God is especially fond of her, and she liked that. I said she puts a smile on God's face and he can't wait to give her a hug and say, "Well done, my daughter."

That went on for a good ten to fifteen minutes. When I finished, she asked if I could text that to my older sister Lucy, so Lucy could read it to her every night before she went to bed. I did that and later emailed it so she could print it out. She's read those words to herself every night since.

Now she talks about having conversations with the Lord. She asks why she hurts in a spot and he tells her. She does what he says and it gets better. She tells her doctors that the Lord is taking care of her. She mentioned a little cough, explaining that it was a little thing, just congestive heart failure. What an outlook on life, amazing. That's my eternally optimistic mom.

———

I hope you'll remember that these words apply to you right now: *God is especially fond of you!* If they touch you deeply, I hope you will forget the shame and condemnation that "church people," or the guy on TV, or whoever, said about you. *You are loved with an everlasting love that knows no bounds.* He has hidden your sins from his sight "as far as the east is from the west." He is slow to remember failings and quick to forgive. He keeps no record of wrongs and smiles down on you from above.[29] And remember that He is with you always, through everything you've

> "God didn't come to forgive sins; He came to forgive sinners and eradicate sin."
> —George MacDonald

---

29. See Psalm 103:8-14

suffered or are suffering. He catches your tears and mixes them with His own. He knows what it's like to suffer, more than any one man or woman, and He shares your burdens.

And if you've given up on him, I ask you to please give Jesus another try. I believe you will find him to be much different than many that claim to follow him. He is anxious to help you find peace and purpose here on this little marble in space we call Earth.

APPENDIX

FAMILY CHRONOLOGY

The following is a record of the names, birth dates, and birthplaces of my immediate biological family—the twenty-seven children who were born to my mother Mildred (Midge), Myra, and Donna. In order to maintain a thread of history, the births are listed in chronological order rather separately for each mother.

Carole Ann (twin) born to Mildred, at Colorado Springs, Colorado, January 6, 1944

Constance Catherine (twin) born to Mildred, at Colorado Springs, January 6, 1944

Lucy Marie, born to Mildred at Short Creek, Arizona, May 22, 1948

Clyde Curtis, born to Mildred at Short Creek, Arizona, August 24, 1950

Seth Morris, born to Donna at Short Creek, Utah, October 3, 1950

Mary Louise, born to Myra at Short Creek, Utah, February 6, 1952

Philip Melvin, born to Mildred at Short Creek, Utah, June 11, 1952

Charlotte, born to Donna at Short Creek, Utah, October 23, 1952

Rowena, born to Myra at Short Creek, Utah, December 18, 1953

Paula Jean, born to Mildred at Short Creek, Utah, February 27, 1954

David Clyde, born to Myra at Short Creek, Utah, October 14, 1955

Howard Calvin, born to Mildred at Short Creek, Utah, October 23, 1955

Shem Lorin, born to Donna at Short Creek, Utah, October 25, 1955

Roberta, born to Mildred at Short Creek, Utah, May 26, 1957

Kathleen Fawn, born to Myra at Short Creek, Utah, October 24, 1957

Karen Lydia, born to Donna at Short Creek, Utah, May 23, 1958

Stan LeRoy, born to Mildred at Short Creek, Utah, January 14, 1959

Stephen Clyde, born to Donna at Short Creek, Utah, May 13, 1960

Paul Chapman, born to Myra at Short Creek, Utah, June 24, 1960

Andrea, born to Mildred at Hildale (near Short Creek) Utah, November 5, 1961

Laura, born to Myra at Hildale, Utah, January 23, 1963

Kenneth Talman, born to Donna at Hildale, Utah, May 20, 1963

Camille, born to Mildred at Salt Lake City, Utah, November 17, 1963

Brian Joseph, born to Myra at Salt Lake City, Utah, January 9, 1967

Mark Owen, born to Donna at Hildale, Utah, September 7, 1967

Maria, born to Donna at Hildale, Utah, April 12, 1970

Melanie, born to Donna at Hildale, Utah, November 6, 1972

AUTHOR'S NOTE

"Imperfection is the beauty of humanity.
Only when we make peace with our failures
can we be free from pretense.
Only then can we be genuine."
—Howard Mackert

Thank you for reading this book. Please email me if you have questions, or perhaps your own story of also coming out of fundamentalism or your own "addiction to certainty." I'd love to hear about your experiences. You can reach me at:

addictedtocertainty.com

. . . or join the conversation by visiting and "liking" my Facebook page.

> Howard is available to speak to your group,
> church, or podcast.

ABOUT THE AUTHOR

Most people in his now-hometown of Gig Harbor, Washington know Howard Mackert as a successful businessman, ace mechanic, generous philanthropist, and active member of the community. What many, if not most, do not know is that Howard is, in his own words, a "twice-recovering fundamentalist."

Howard grew up, until the age of twenty-five, in a polygamous fundamentalist Mormon (FLDS) family in Arizona and later Utah. As a young man, he realized the frustration and powerlessness of his situation, and courageously separated himself and set out on his own. (This departure was *after* Howard achieved the distinction of being a twenty-five-year-old divorced virgin!)

Through the ups and downs chronicled in this book, Howard found his way first to Christian fundamentalism, still looking for the security of having someone provide him with the "certainty" and dogmatic answers he thought he needed. It was not long before he realized that this situation, too, was problematic.

Through it all, Howard's upbeat, optimistic personality and no-nonsense approach to life and spirituality led him, ultimately, to a life-changing divine encounter and an entirely new worldview, one of *love* and *grace*. After that, there was no turning back, and since then Howard has devoted himself to living outside the box of legalism and inside the embrace of a loving Heavenly Father whose unconditional love erases the lines many want to draw around Him.

Besides his leadership role at Mackert Automotive, of which he is the owner and president, Howard is actively involved in many community and charity endeavors, and is a frequently sought-out speaker. He is also an enthusiastic supporter of his wife Rhonda in her music career. Howard and Rhonda make their home in Gig Harbor, Washington, with their two beautiful Keeshonds, Mieke and Keelin.

CPSIA information can be obtained
at www.ICGtesting.com
Printed in the USA
LVHW082221210220
647690LV00001B/1